I0908295

# The Tofu Gourmet

# The Tofu Gourmet

by L. Barber & J. Lampert

SHUFUNOTOMO / JAPAN PUBLICATIONS

First printing, 1984

Photographs by Shufunotomo Co., Ltd.
Book design by Momoyo Nishimura

Published by SHUFUNOTOMO CO., LTD.
1-6, Kanda Surugadai, Chiyoda-ku, Tokyo, 101 Japan


Distributors:
UNITED STATES: Kodansha International/USA, Ltd.,
through Harper & Row, Publishers, Inc., 10 East 53rd
Street, New York, New York 10022.
Canada: Fitzenry & Whiteside Ltd., 150 Lesmill Road,
Don Mills, Ontario M3b2T6.


ISBN: 0-87040-589-6
Printed in Japan

# Preface

To a gourmet, cooking and eating is an art. The selection, preparation, presentation of a food is a total sensual experience to be enjoyed and savored. It is this kind of feeling that Junko and I wanted to be portrayed throughout this book on tofu cookery.

Before one can be a true tofu gourmet, knowledge about tofu, or soybean curd as it is sometimes called, is necessary. Originally an Oriental food, tofu is now made throughout the world. Basically the same method has been used for over 2000 years. Tofu is made by grinding soaked soybeans and boiling the resulting purée. After straining the purée, this soymilk is curdled. The curds are gently ladled into forming boxes and pressed to form the white cake we know as "tofu."

Over the years, tofu had made a name for itself because it is a nutritious food. High in protein, low in saturated fats and sodium, tofu is a good food for everyone. But tofu is not only a healthful food. When you taste fresh tofu directly from the package you will understand why people are turning into tofu epicures. Being very mild in taste in itself, tofu can be flavored and styled into a variety of culinary pleasures.

If you are unfamiliar with tofu as an ingredient this book will guide you to some simple, yet glamourous food delights. And for those of you who know and love tofu, this book will give you some new and fresh ways to serve tofu to family and friends. After trying a few of these recipes we think you will agree that tofu is a food for gourmets, and cooking with tofu a true epicurean experience.

Linda L. Barber
Madison, Wisconsin

Junko Lampert
Tokyo, Japan

# Contents

Measurement
1 oz.  : 28.53 g
1 lb.  : 453.59 g
1 kg.  : 2.2 lbs.
1 cup  : 250 cc

4

★ Recipes without illustrations.

# Ways To Prepare Tofu

Before trying any recipe in this book you should acquaint yourself with some basic tofu preparation techniques. Throughout this book, six methods are used: steaming, scrambling, pressing, puréeing or blending, parboiling and draining. All of these techniques are described below.

## Steaming

**Purpose:**
Steaming heats tofu quickly without losing water soluable vitamins and minerals. Also, because no fat is necessary for cooking, this method is a wonderful way to prepare tofu for the fat conscious.

**Method:**
Almost any deep pot with a tight fitting lid can be turned into a steamer by placing a baking rack or colander on the bottom of the pot, thus keeping the tofu above the liquid, not in it. Many cooks use a heat-proof plate instead of a rack and rest it on a metal ring (made by removing the top and bottom of a tuna can). Follow the specific recipe for correct steaming time.

## Scrambling

**Purpose:**
This method causes the tofu to give up liquid whey. After scrambling, tofu will resemble the texture of cottage cheese and be slightly firm.

**Method:**
Place tofu in a saucepan or skillet. Sprinkle with salt (optional). Cook over medium heat, stirring with a wooden spoon, breaking tofu into small pieces as you stir. After about 5 minutes tofu will resemble cottage cheese and whey will be separate from the curds. Pour contents into a cloth lined colander. Drain. Allow to cool at room temperature. Some recipes suggest you gather the cloth corners to form a sack and twist close. Using your hands, twist to expel as much whey as possible.

## Pressing

**Purpose:**
By pressing tofu, water is expelled, causing tofu to become firm, yet the shape is preserved.

**Methods:**
Two different methods for pressing tofu are used in this book—The Towel and Refrigerator Method and The Pressing Method.
**The Towel and Refrigerator Method:** Wrap tofu in a folded cotton kitchen towel and set on a plate in the refrigerator for the time specified in the recipe.
**The Pressing Method:** Wrap tofu in a folded cotton kitchen towel and place on a cutting board, cookie sheet or a large plate next to the sink. Raise the far end of the board several inches and place another cutting board or plate atop the wrapped tofu. Set a 1–2 pound weight (canned goods work well) on the board. Let stand 15 minutes, or as recipe directs.

## Puréeing or Blending

**Purpose:**
One of the most popular ways to prepare tofu, blending transforms tofu into a creamy, smooth product suitable for dips, spreads, soups, sauces, dressings and desserts.

# Buying
# and Storing Tofu

**Method:**

For easier blending, pour liquid ingredients into the blender first. Add tofu a little at a time so as not to overwork the blender's motor.

You may also blend tofu without liquids by slowly puréeing tofu a little at a time, scraping the tofu to the center of the blender jar with a rubber spatula while the motor is turned off.

## Parboiling

**Purpose:**

This technique serves many purposes: 1) warms tofu; 2) freshens stored tofu that shows signs of spoiling; 3) firms up tofu; and 4) flavors tofu if parboiled in a flavored broth or salted water.

**Method:**

Add tofu to boiling water. Reduce heat and cover. Continue heating for a few minutes or until tofu is warmed.

## Draining

**Purpose:**

Draining tofu produces a firm product and since it is out of water it also preserves tofu's natural sweetness. This method is used when tofu is to be cooked in flavored broth.

**Method:**

Place tofu in a colander that is placed over a bowl or container. Cover and place in the refrigerator for 1 or 2 hours or as recipe directs.

Even though tofu is a vegetable product, it does spoil quickly. Look for tofu in the refrigerated section of your supermarket. Since fresh tofu tastes best, purchase the container with the latest date stamp. Fresh tofu is creamy white, has little or no odor. The package should not be swollen, nor the contents foamy.

After purchasing tofu, remove it from the package, put it in another container and cover with fresh water. Cover with foil or plastic wrap. Keep tofu refrigerated. Change the tofu's water daily. Stored this way, tofu will keep 2–3 days.

Tofu may be stored indefinitely in the freezer. During the freezing process, tofu changes from a creamy to a chewy meatlike texture. To freeze tofu simply drain and wrap well. Freeze. When ready to use, thaw, squeeze out the excess liquid, and crumble or cube. Although no recipe for frozen tofu is given in this book, you may want to create your own Tofu Gourmet Special by adding frozen tofu to your favorite stew, soup or casserole instead of the usual meat, chicken or fish.

If tofu has to be kept fresh for a longer time, parboil tofu for 5 minutes in water to which a little salt has been added. Drain and store as directed above. It will stay fresh for 4–5 days.

# PART I

10–11      14–17      18      20

30      32      34      36

46      48      50      52

62      64      66      68

22

24

26

28

38

40

42

44

54

56

58

60

70

72

74

76–79

# Tofu Mushroom Dip

Also good as sandwich spread.

**Ingredients:**
1¼ cups (300 g) tofu
2 tablespoons minced onion
½ cup (⅛ l) heavy cream
½ teaspoon pepper
1 bouillon cube, dissolved in ¼ cup (60 ml) hot water
7 oz. (200 g) fresh mushrooms, wiped clean and stemmed
1 tablespoon butter
½ teaspoon salt

**Method:**
1. Wrap tofu in a cloth and let stand for 20 minutes. Then purée in a blender.
2. Add onion, heavy cream, pepper, soup and purée again.
3. Finely mince mushrooms and fry in butter until soft. Season with salt and stir into tofu mixture.
4. Serve with fresh vegetables or crackers.

Makes about 3 cups dip.

# Tofu Blue Cheese Dip

A pungent party treat

**Ingredients:**
1¼ cups (300 g) tofu
½ cup (120 g) blue cheese
½ cup (⅛ l) sour cream
½ teaspoon salt
¼ teaspoon pepper

**Method:**
1. Wrap tofu in a cloth and let stand for 20 minutes.
2. Combine all ingredients in a blender and purée until very smooth.
3. Serve with vegetable sticks.

Makes about 2½ cups dip.

# Spinach Dip

Serve this dip in a hollowed out round loaf of rye bread. Surround the stuffed loaf with bread cubes (from the loaf's center) and a selection of fresh vegetables or crackers.

**Ingredients:**
1 cup (225 g) mashed tofu
¼ teaspoon dry mustard
½ teaspoon salt
3 tablespoons vinegar
½ cup (⅛ l) salad oil
½ cup (70 g) chopped green onions
½ cup (35 g) chopped parsley
One 10 ounce (280 g) package frozen spinach, thawed, squeezed and coarsely chopped

**Method:**
1. Combine first 5 ingredients in a blender until smooth. Pour into a medium size bowl.
2. Stir in remaining ingredients.
3. Serve immediately, or cover and refrigerate until ready to serve.

Makes about 3 cups dip.

# Curry Dip

Delicious with fresh vegetables or fruit.

**Ingredients:**
½ teaspoon dry mustard
1½ teaspoons curry powder
½ cup (120 g) Tofu Mayonnaise
    (see page 74)
½ teaspoon vinegar
1½ teaspoons honey

**Method:**
1.  Mix all ingredients in a blender until smooth.
2.  For best flavor, serve chilled.

Makes about ½ cup dip.

# Party Dip

For a glamorous party tray fill avocado halves with this dip and surround with crackers.

**Ingredients:**
1–3 oz. (90 g) package cream cheese
1 cup (225 g) mashed tofu
1¾ cups (175 ml) yogurt
½ teaspoon salt
1 tablespoon chopped parsley
1 tablespoon minced onion

**Method:**
1.  Mix cheese, tofu, yogurt and salt together in a blender until smooth.
2.  By hand, stir in parsley and onion.
3.  Serve as suggested above, or pour dip into a bowl and surround with fresh vegetables for dipping.

Makes about 2 cups dip.

# Tofu Tuna Dip

Vary the amount of tuna to your taste.

**Ingredients:**
1¼ cups (300 g) tofu
1 can (about 160 g solid weight) flaked tuna, drained
3 tablespoons minced onion
2 teaspoons hot mustard
2 teaspoons paprika
5–6 drops tabasco
3 tablespoons lemon juice
1 tablespoon fine herbs
Salt and pepper

**Method:**
1.  Wrap tofu in a cloth and let stand for 15 minutes. Then purée in a blender.
2.  Add all the other ingredients except for salt and pepper and blend until smooth.
3.  Season with salt and pepper, if necessary. Serve with vegetable sticks.

Makes about 3 cups dip.

# Tofu Party Canapés

Served on a silver plate, the colorful canapés will enhance the party atmosphere

**Ingredients:**
1¼ lb. (600 g) tofu, pressed
Flour for dredging
Salt and white pepper
Salad oil for frying
For garnish:
    Cheese, caviar, chicken spread, cottage cheese, tomato slices, anchovies, tuna flakes, fried bacon, minced chives, boiled shrimps, etc.

**Method:**
1.  Cut tofu into slices about 1 × 2 inches (2.5 × 5 cm) and ¼ inch (7 mm) thick. Sprinkle with salt and pepper.
2.  Dredge tofu with flour and fry on both · sides until crisp bown.
3.  Arrange grilled tofu on a warmed plate. Decorate with garnishes of your choice and serve warm.

**Cold Canapés**
Spread tofu slices over a dish cloth. Sprinkle with 1 tablespoon salt and let stand for 30 minutes.

Decorate with garnishes and keep cool until serving time. You can garnish cold canapés with fresh fruit, avocado slices or marinated fish.

# Tofu Mushroom Terrine

It takes time to make this dish, but it is really worth trying.

**Ingredients:**
9 oz. (250 g) veal
½ teaspoon salt
A dash of pepper
1 teaspoon paprika powder
1 lb. and 1 oz. (500 g) tofu
1 lb. and 10 oz. (750 g) fresh mushrooms or
    1 lb. (480 g net weight) canned
    mushrooms, drained.

4 oz. (100 g) pork fat, cut into small pieces
    (optional)
3 tablespoons salad oil
½ cup minced shallot or onion
4 tablespoons brandy
½ cup (50 g) bread crumbs
½ cup (120 ml) heavy cream
9 oz. (250 g) bacon or enough to cover the
    whole terrine
3 sticks crabmeat

**Method:**
1. Remove all the tough parts from the veal. Cut into small pieces. Season with salt, pepper and paprika. Set aside.
2. Wrap tofu in a large cloth and press for 15 minutes.
3. Meanwhile, clean and wash mushrooms under running water. Drain in a colander.
4. Heat oil in a frying pan. Sauté onion and mushrooms for 5 minutes. Add brandy and bring back to a boil. Drain and let cool.
5. To make stuffing: In a blender combine all ingredients except for mushrooms and bacon. Blend until smooth. If the blender is not powerful enough process in two or three portions.
6. Line bottom and wall of a terrine with bacon. Fill with ⅓ of the stuffing. Layer one half of the mushroom mixture. Distribute evenly. Repeat the process. Place crabmeat or other colorful ingredients in the center as decoration.
7. Fill with the last ⅓ of the farce. Smooth the surface with a spatula. Cover tightly with bacon slices.
8. Heat oven to 325°F. (160°C.). Fill a shallow pan to ⅓ of its height with water. Place the terrine in the pan and bake covered 45 minutes. To test doneness press with your fingers center part of the terrine. When the terrine springs back, it is done. Take out of the oven and let stand for at least 2 hours to set.
9. Cut in slices to serve.

**Note:**
Do not soak mushrooms in water. They should not become soggy. Wash them quickly under running water. Drain thoroughly.

# Easy Tofu Liver Spread

**Ingredients:**
10 oz. (300 g) tofu
¼ cup minced onion
10 oz. (300 g) pork liver
½ lb. (225 g) ground meat (beef, pork or chicken)
3 tablespoons salad oil
1 bouillon cube
½ teaspoon salt
¼ teaspoon black pepper
1 tablespoon oregano
1 tablespoon sweet thyme or fine herbs
¼ cup brandy
2 tablespoons cornstarch
¼–½ cup (120 g) heavy cream (optional)

**Method:**
1. Wrap tofu in a cloth and let stand for 15 minutes.
2. Clean liver, wash out blood with cold water and pat dry.
3. Sauté onion in oil for a few minutes. Add liver and ground meat. Brown well.
4. Add tofu, seasonings and spices and bring to a boil, stirring from time to time.
5. Pour brandy over and flame.
6. Sprinkle cornstarch over mixture. Cook another 3 minutes, stirring constantly. Cover the skillet and simmer for a few minutes. Then uncover and cook over medium heat until the liquid is reduced to one half.
7. Turn heat off and let cool for 15 minutes.
8. Pour the contents of the skillet into a blender and blend to desired smoothness. Add heavy cream, if you like a lighter color. (Adding cream makes the consistency thinner.)

Makes about 4 cups spread. It keeps about 1 week in a refrigerator. Freeze it in portions for up to 2 months.

# Trout Spread

You can substitute almost any smoked fish for the trout.

**Ingredients:**
1¼ cups (300 g) tofu
3 fillets of smoked trout (5–6 oz., 150–180 g)
¼ cup (60 ml) salad oil
3 tablespoons vinegar
1 teaspoon hot mustard
½ teaspoon salt
A dash of pepper
3 tablespoons chopped capers, minced pickles or minced onion as garnish

**Method:**
1. In a saucepan crumble tofu. Bring to a boil. Cook over high heat for 2 minutes, stirring constantly. Do not let tofu become dry and yellowish.
2. Press in a cloth sack to expel moisture.
3. In a blender, combine all ingredients and mix until blended, scraping the wall of the blender with a spatula from time to time.
4. Serve with chopped capers, minced pickles and onion.

Makes about 2½ cups spread.

# Okara Crackers

These are fun to make on a snowbound afternoon.

**Ingredients:**
1¼ cups (175 g) packed okara
1 cup (140 g) whole wheat flour
½ cup (70 g) wheat germ
1 teaspoon salt
½ cup (⅛ l) salad oil
3 tablespoons mashed tofu

**Method:**
1. Mix all ingredients together.
2. Knead dough until smooth (about 5 minutes)
3. Roll dough between 2 sheets of wax paper until it is ⅛ inch (3 mm) thick.
4. Cut dough into shapes using cooky cutters. Place crackers on baking sheets and bake at 325°F. (160°C.) for about 10 minutes, or until crackers are light brown and crisp.
5. Cool, and store in an airtight container.

Makes about 60 crackers.

Vary cracker flavors by adding one of the following to the dough:
½ teaspoon curry
¼ cup (60 g) grated Parmesan cheese
¼ cup shredded coconut
¼ cup (70 g) sesame, caraway, or poppy seeds

# Okaraola

Serve with yogurt, or milk and fruit for a healthful breakfast.

**Ingredients:**
3 cups (240 g) oatmeal
½ cup (70 g) wheat germ
½ cup (60 g) toasted sesame seeds
½ cup (130 g) sliced almonds
3¾ cups (325 g) packed okara
2 tablespoons cinnamon
⅔ cup (170 ml) water
⅔ cup (226 g) honey
⅔ cup (160 ml) salad oil
1 cup raisins

**Method:**
1. Mix oatmeal, wheat germ, sesame seeds, almonds, packed okara and cinnamon together in a large bowl. Set aside.
2. In a saucepan stir water, salad oil and honey together. Heat until blended.
3. Pour hot honey mixture over the okara mixture. Stir until dry ingredients are moist.
4. Spread cereal on 2 large baking sheets and bake at 325°F. (160°C.) for about 25 minutes. Stir every 10 minutes until mixture is dry and light brown in color.
5. Cool, then stir in raisins before packing cereal into airtight containers.

Makes about 7 cups cereal or 28 servings.

**Note:**
This cereal is very filling, the dry okara swells in your stomach. One fourth cup is enough to keep any stomach happy!

# All Purpose Tofu Sauce

Use this sauce as salad dressing or for cold meat slices. Warmed up it goes very nicely with spaghetti and cooked vegetables.

**Ingredients:**
1¼ cups (300 g) tofu
3 tablespoons ground sesame seeds or sesame butter
½ cup (⅛ l) fresh cream
1 tablespoon miso
2 teaspoons salt
¼ teaspoon pepper
3 tablespoons ketchup
4 tablespoons brandy
3 tablespoons salad oil
½ cup (⅛ l) soup stock

**Method:**
1. Wrap tofu in a cloth and let stand for 15 minutes.
2. Combine all ingredients in a blender and mix until very smooth.

Makes about 3 cups sauce.

**Variation:**
Omit sesame seeds and use ½ cup ground walnuts.

# Tofu Cheese Sauce

Leftover refrigerated sauce firms up to make a delightful cheese spread for crackers or celery sticks.

**Ingredients:**
⅔ cup (160 ml) milk
1½ cups (300 g) tofu
¼ teaspoon salt
¼ teaspoon dry mustard
¼ teaspoon paprika
A pinch of freshly ground pepper
1½ cups (200 g) shredded natural cheddar cheese

**Method:**
1. Mix milk, tofu, salt and spices together in a blender until smooth. Pour mixture into a saucepan.
2. Add the shredded cheese and stir over low heat until cheese is melted. If the mixture becomes lumpy, return it to the blender and mix until smooth.
3. Serve over steamed vegetables or over pasta.

Makes about 2 cups.

# Tofu White Sauce

A white sauce that even dieters can enjoy!

**Ingredients:**
⅔ cups (160 ml) milk
1½ cups (300 g) tofu
½ teaspoon salt
¼ teaspoon dry mustard
¼ teaspoon paprika
A pinch of freshly ground pepper
1 tablespoon butter or margarine (optional)

**Method:**
1. Mix all ingredients in a blender until smooth.
2. Pour into a saucepan and heat, but don't boil! Overcooking will curdle the sauce. If sauce should separate, return it to the blender jar and mix until smooth.
3. Serve over steamed vegetables, or use as you would regular white sauce.

Makes about 2 cups.

# Okara Marrow Pie and Tarts

Serve warm, with a glass of red wine.

**Ingredients:**
For crust:
  1½ cups (250 g) flour
  1 stick (125 g) butter
  1 small egg or 1 egg white
  2 tablespoons cold water
  A pinch of salt
For filling:
  1 cup (88 g) bread crumbs (or 5 slices
    white bread)
  1 cup (¼ l) milk
  2 oz. (50 g) marrow (about the size of a
    golfball)
  ½ cup (70 g) okara
  A pinch of salt, pepper and nutmeg
  1 egg
To glaze the pie:
  1 egg yolk

**Method:**
1. In a bowl combine all the ingredients for
   crust except the water.
2. With a pastry blender mix quickly to
   form a smooth dough, adding water little by little.
3. Wrap in foil and chill in refrigerator for
   at least 2 hours.
4. In a bowl flake the marrow into fine
   crumbs, using a fork. Set aside.
5. Soak bread crumbs in the milk, then
   press and squeeze out moisture. Set
   aside.
6. Add okara, egg and seasonings, and
   soaked bread to the marrow. Knead to
   form a smooth dough.
7. Butter brioche molds or small tartlet
   molds. Roll out pastry dough ⅕ inch (5
   mm) thick. Line the molds with pastry
   dough. Fill with okara-marrow filling.
   Cover with pastry dough and trim off
   excess pastry along the edge of the mold.
8. Brush with beaten egg yolk and bake in
   moderate oven 25–30 minutes. Serve
   hot.

Makes about 5 tarts of 3½-inch (8.5 cm)
mold or 8 tarts of 2½-inch (6 cm) mold.

# Tofu Knishes

**Ingredients:**
Knish-crust:
  ½ cup (130 g) mashed potatoes
  2 tablespoons salad oil
  ½ teaspoon salt
  1¼ cups (170 g) all purpose flour
  ½ teaspoon baking powder
  ¼ cup (⅛ l) water
Filling:
  ¼ lb. (112 g) cabbage chopped into
    ½-inch (1.2 cm) chunks (approximately
    1 cup)
  ¼ onion, chopped into chunks
  1 tablespoon salad oil
  1 cup (250 g) mashed tofu
  1 tablespoon shoyu (soy sauce)
  ½ teaspoon ginger
  ½ teaspoon minced garlic
  ¼ teaspoon curry powder

**Method:**
Knish-crust:
1. Mix potatoes, oil and salt until combined.
2. Add flour, baking powder and water.
   Mix until smooth.
3. Knead dough until smooth. Let dough
   rest for 30 minutes while preparing the
   filling.

Filling:
1. Sauté cabbage and onions until soft.
2. Add tofu, shoyu, ginger, garlic and curry. Set aside to cool.

Knishes:
1. Pinch off small pieces of dough, ¾ inch
   (1.8 cm) in diameter, and roll into 4-inch
   (10 cm) circles about ⅛ inch (3 mm)
   thick.
2. Place a spoonful of filling in the center of
   the dough circle, fold over, and pinch
   the edges together.
3. Place knishes on a greased baking pan,
   seam side up, and bake at 375°F. (190°C.)
   for about 25 minutes, or until knishes are
   light brown.
4. Serve hot or cold.

*(Tofu Knishes are illustrated in color on page 29.)*

# Vegetable Quiche

Vary this recipe by using other vegetables instead of the sautéed onions. Steam the vegetables before pouring the filling.

**Ingredients:**
3 medium onions, sliced
2 tablespoons salad oil
4 eggs
1 lb. (450 g) tofu
1½ teaspoons salt
¼ teaspoon pepper
2 cups (260 g) shredded cheese
1 9-inch (22 cm) pie crust (page 116)
Broccoli, steamed for garnish

**Method:**
1. Sauté onion slices in oil until soft and transparent. Set aside.
2. Mix eggs, tofu, salt and pepper together in a blender until smooth. By hand, stir in the shredded cheese.
3. Distribute onions on the bottom of the pie shell. Pour tofu mixture over onions. Decorate with steamed broccoli pieces.
4. Bake at 350°F. (180°C.) for 45 minutes or until a knife inserted in the quiche comes out clean.
5. Serve cut in wedges either hot or cold.

Makes one 9-inch (23 cm) quiche.

# Creamed Tofu

Serve over rice, toast points, puff paste or use as a filling for crêpes.

**Ingredients:**
¼ cup (50 g) butter or margarine
1 medium onion, diced
1 cup (140 g) sliced mushrooms
1 clove garlic, minced
¼ cup (35 g) all purpose flour
1½ cups (375 ml) milk
1 tablespoon minced parsley
¼ teaspoon thyme
½ teaspoon salt
Dash of pepper
¼ cup (65 ml) white wine
1 cup (140 g) frozen green peas
1½ cups (300 g) cubed tofu (cut tofu into ¾-inch (1.8 cm) cubes)

**Method:**
1. Sauté onion, mushroom and garlic in butter until transparent.
2. Add flour and stir constantly.
3. Add milk and cook over low flame until sauce is thick and creamy.
4. Add parsley, thyme, salt, pepper and wine.
5. Gently stir in peas and tofu cubes. Cook until heated.
6. Serve hot as suggested above.

Makes 3 servings.

# Man's Cake

An eye-catcher on the party table!

**Ingredients:**
2 lb. (750–900 g) tofu
A:
    2 tablespoons paprika powder
    5–6 drops tabasco
    ½ teaspoon salt
    ¼ teaspoon pepper
    4 tablespoons tomato paste
    1 tablespoon very finely minced onion
B:
    ¼ teaspoon pepper
    2 tablespoons very finely minced chives
    2 tablespoons very finely minced parsley
    and other herbs of your choice (tarra-
    gon, basil, chervil, borage, mint, etc.)
C:
    ½ teaspoon salt
    ¼ teaspoon pepper
    2 tablespoons finely chopped onion
    2 teaspoons hot mustard
    2 hardboiled eggs, minced
    2 tablespoons mayonnaise
For shortcrust:
    2⅔ cups (400 g) flour
    1 cup (200 g) butter
    1 small egg
    A pinch of salt
    3 tablespoons cold water
For garnish:
Alfalfa sprouts
Carrots, radishes

**Method:**
1. Prepare short crust pastries (page 116).
   Rest 2 hours in a refrigerator.
2. Divide dough into three equal portions.
   Roll out one portion out into circle about
   ⅕ inch (5 mm) thick. Place a
   plate of 10-inch (25 cm) diameter on it
   and using a knife, trim the crust sticking
   out of the plate. Bake until crisp.
3. Prepare other portions of the dough to
   make 3 round pastries.
4. Crumble tofu into a saucepan, add 2
   teaspoons salt and cook for 3 minutes.
   Drain onto a large dry cloth. Fold the
   ends of the cloth tightly and press to expel moisture. Then divide tofu into 3
   equal portions and set aside.
5. Combine one portion of tofu with the
   ingredients A and mix well.
6. Proceed with the other two portions of
   tofu with ingredients B and C.
7. Spread the pastries with tofu spreads
   (each with different taste) and place them
   in layers.
8. Decorate with alfalfa sprouts, shredded
   carrot and radishes.

Makes a 10-inch (25 cm) cake or 12–16 servings.

# Cream of Tofu Soup

Mild and refreshing.

**Ingredients:**
1 cup (250 g) tofu
1 teaspoon salt
1½ cups (¼ l + ⅛ l) milk
2 bouillon cubes
2 tablespoons cornstarch
½ cup (⅛ l) heavy cream
Chopped chives as garnish

**Method:**
1. Purée tofu together with salt in a blender until smooth.
2. In a saucepan bring milk to a boil. Crumble soup cubes into the milk and stir till they dissolve.
3. Dissolve cornstarch in a little cold water, add to the milk and cook for 2 minutes until thickened, stirring constantly.
4. Add heavy cream and tofu purée and cook until warm; do not boil.
5. Garnish with chives and serve in bowls.

Serves 4.

# Tofu Pumpkin Soup

A creamed vegetable that will delight the children.

**Ingredients:**
2 cups (500 g) pumpkin (or winter squash)
1¼ cups (300 g) tofu
1 bouillon cube
1 cup (¼ l) water
1½ cups (¼ l + ⅛ l) cold milk
2 tablespoons cornstarch
1 teaspoon salt
Chopped chives as garnish

**Method:**
1. Peel pumpkin, discard seeds and slice thinly.
2. Cook in water with bouillon cube until tender.
3. Blend tofu together with cooked pumpkin in a blender until very smooth.
4. Dissolve cornstarch in a little cold water. In a saucepan bring milk to a boil, add cornstarch and cook until thickened, stirring constantly to avoid burning.
5. Add the tofu-pumpkin purée and mix thoroughly. Bring back to a boil. Season with salt.
6. Sprinkle chives over the soup and serve.

Serves 6.

**Variation:**
Instead of pumpkin, use green peas, cooked white beans, carrots or potatoes.

# Tofu Marrow Dumplings

Marrow gives a full taste to the soup. Serve hot with garlic toast previous to a fish dish. Or add vegetables to the soup and it will make a heart warming winter treat.

**Ingredients:**
10½ oz. (300 g) tofu
Marrow from 2 lb. (1 kg) of beef bone
  (about 1 cup loosely measured)
1 egg
2 tablespoons flour
1 teaspoon salt
2 tablespoons minced parsley
8 cups (2 l) water
2 bay leaves
5 peppercorns
Okra for garnish

**Method:**
1. Press tofu with a heavy weight for 20 minutes, then crumble.
2. Place marrow in a colander and let water run over it to remove blood stains and dirt. You can omit this stage if the marrow is clean.
3. Mash marrow finely with a fork.
4. Combine tofu, marrow, parsley, egg and salt in a bowl. Mix thoroughly. Add flour little by little only until the dough is firm enough to form balls.
5. Bring water to a boil. Add bay leaves and peppercorns.
6. Hold a little dough in your hand, close the fingers gently to press a small ball out of the opening made by thumb and forefinger into the boiling water, then turn the heat down immediately and let simmer for 20 minutes.
7. Try one ball to see if it is cooked through. If not, cook a little longer.
8. Strain the broth and correct seasoning with salt and pepper. Place 5–7 marrow balls into individual soup bowls. Pour clear broth over them and garnish with chopped okra. Serve immediately.

**Variation:**
You can add coarsely chopped cooked vegetables (like celery, carrot and onion) to the soup to make a light meal out of the marrow soup. Serve with whole wheat toast and a green salad.

# Tofu Chicken Dumplings

So soft that they melt in your mouth.

**Ingredients:**
1 cup (250 g) ground chicken meat
1 tablespoon cornstarch
2 tablespoons minced onion
1¼ cups (300 g) tofu, pressed and crumbled
½ teaspoon salt
¼ teaspoon pepper
Chicken broth or any other kind of clear
   soup
Parsley or sliced okra for garnish

**Method:**
1. Combine all the ingredients (except soup stock and parsley) in a bowl and mix until blended. Set aside.
2. In a large pot bring 8 cups of water to a boil. Add 1 tablespoon salt.
3. With a wooden spatula scoop out a little dough, scrape off with a wet rubber spatula to make small dumplings of about 1-inch (2.5 cm) length one after another into the boiling water, rinsing the rubber spatula with cold water as soon as it begins to stick. As dumplings cook, they will rise to the surface. Stop forming new dumplings when the whole surface is covered with dumplings. Let simmer for 5 more minutes and then take the dumplings out of the water with a slotted spoon and place in a warm bowl. Keep covered.
4. Repeat the process with the rest of the dough.
5. Warm the chicken broth. Correct seasoning, if necessary. Place 5–7 dumplings in individual soup bowls. Pour hot broth over them. Sprinkle with minced parsley and serve immediately.

# Tofu Potato Dumplings

Add leftover vegetables and ham, and it will make a hearty meal.

**Ingredients:**
1¼ cups (300 g) tofu, pressed and crumbled
3 medium-sized potatoes, grated and well drained
1 egg
2 tablespoons flour
½ cup (30 g) minced parsley
Salt and pepper to taste

**Method:**
1. Combine tofu, grated potatoes, flour, egg and parsley in a blender until smooth. Season with salt and pepper.
2. Form dumplings about the thickness of a finger 1½ inches (4 cm) long, using two wet spoons. Cook them in boiling water for about 15 minutes or until done. (Take a bite to test if the potatoes have become soft and the dumpling has a smooth texture. If not, cook a little longer).
3. Serve dumplings in a clear soup or as accompaniment to a meat dish with gravy.

# Baked Fish with Tofu Sauce

A tangy white sauce creates a glamorous casserole. If you are in a hurry omit baking and just pour warm sauce over the fish.

**Ingredients:**

1 cup (¼ l) water
1 cup (¼ l) dry white wine
Juice of ½ lemon
2 bay leaves
1 small onion, sliced
1 tablespoon + 1 teaspoon (20 ml) brandy
5 peppercorns
1 teaspoon salt
2 lb. 4 oz. (1 kg) fish fillets (cod, bass, halibut, etc.)
12 oz. (350 g) fresh spinach leaves
For the white sauce:
   1¼ cups (300 g) tofu
   3 tablespoons butter
   3 tablespoons flour
   2 cups (½ l) fish stock
   1 cup (¼ l) milk
   Juice of ½ lemon
   1 teaspoon salt
   A dash of pepper
   3 tablespoons chopped dill weed

**Method:**

1. Blend tofu in a blender until smooth. Set aside.
2. Combine water, wine, lemon juice, bay leaves, onions, brandy, peppercorns and salt in a large pan. Bring to a boil.
3. Place fish fillets into the boiling water, reduce heat and cook over low heat for 15 minutes.
4. Remove fish fillets and keep warm.
5. Strain stock and keep warm.
6. Parboil spinach in salted water, drain and cut into bite-size pieces. Set aside.
7. Melt butter in a frying pan. Add flour and cook for 2 minutes, stirring constantly with a wooden spoon to avoid burning. Add fish stock, milk, salt, pepper and cook over low heat until thick and smooth. Remove from heat.
8. Add tofu purée and lemon to the white sauce. Mix thoroughtly.
9. Preheat oven to 400°F. (200°C.). Butter a gratin dish, cover the bottom with cooked fish, spread chopped spinach over it, and pour the white sauce over all. Sprinkle with dill. Bake in the oven until the sauce begins to bubble and the top is browned.

# Pork Pie with Tofu Mousse

Served hot or cold, it will satisfy the most fastidious gourmet.

## Ingredients:

For pie crust:
- 1½ cups + 3 tablespoons (250 g) flour
- 1 stick (125 g) butter
- 1 small egg
- A pinch of salt
- 2 tablespoons cold water

For mousse:
- 1¼ cups (250 g) tofu
- 1½ cups (200 g) mushrooms, wiped clean, stemmed and minced
- 2 tablespoons cornstarch
- ¼ cup (35 g) minced shallots or onion
- ½ teaspoon salt
- A dash of black pepper
- ¼ cup (65 ml) brandy
- ½ cup (40 g) bread crumbs
- 1 egg white
- ½ teaspoon thyme
- 3 tablespoons minced parsley

1 lb. (450 g) pork steak
Salt and pepper
4 tablespoons salad oil
1 egg yolk

## Method:

1. To make the pie crust follow the instruction on page 116. Chill at least 2 hours.
2. In a saucepan crumble tofu with ½ teaspoon salt. Bring to a boil. Cook over high heat for 3 minutes. Pour into a cloth sack and press firmly to expel as much moisture as possible. Set aside.
3. Sauté shallot in oil until translucent. Add mushrooms and sauté another 3 minutes. Sprinkle brandy over them and bring back to a boil. Add cornstarch, dissolved in a little water, and cook for 1 minute. Set aside.
4. Season pork steak with a little salt and black pepper. Heat a small amount of oil in a frying pan and brown fillet over high heat on all sides. Set aside.
5. Combine tofu, mushrooms, bread crumbs, egg white, thyme and parsley in a bowl. Mix with a fork or by hand until blended. Tofu should be crumbled to small pieces.
6. Divide pastry dough into 2 parts, one piece double the size of the other. Roll out both pieces of dough ⅛ inch (3 mm) thick into an oval shape.
7. Spread ½ of the tofu mousse over the smaller pastry, leaving ⅔-inch (1.6 cm) edge free all around. Place fillet in center. Cover with the rest of the tofu mixture. Pat smooth.
8. Place the other pastry over the loaf, close it completely by pressing the dough tightly all around the loaf. Cut off the excess dough.
9. Brush the pastry with egg yolk. Make ribbons out of the leftover dough. Decorate the pastry and brush with egg yolk again. Let stand for 20 minutes to set.
10. Preheat oven to 375°F. (190°C.) and bake the pie for 25–30 minutes until golden brown.

## Chicken Fillets with Tofu Curry Stuffing

Combination of mild chicken meat with spicy filling is loved by everyone.

**Ingredients:**
1¼ cups (300 g) tofu, well pressed
4 breast fillets of chicken, about 7 oz.
  (200 g each)
⅓ cup (80 g) minced parsley
⅓ cup (80 g) minced celery
⅓ cup (60 g) minced onion
1 egg
1 teaspoon salt
A pinch of pepper
1 tablespoon curry powder
1 egg
½ cup (100 g) all purpose flour
1 cup (88 g) bread crumbs
Salad oil for deep-frying

**Method:**
1. With a sharp knife cut a slit into chicken fillets to make pouches. Set aside.
2. Crumble tofu in a bowl. Add parsley, celery, onion, ⅓ cup bread crumbs and egg. Season with salt, pepper and curry. Mix thoroughly.
3. Fill the chicken pouches with the stuffing, leaving ½ inch (12 mm) of the edge free.
4. Press the stuffed pouch lightly between your hands to close the edge and to distribute the stuffing evenly.
5. Coat the stuffed chicken first with flour, then dip in beaten egg. Then roll in bread crumbs.
6. Heat oil in a deep skillet to cover the chicken pieces and fry 10 minutes over medium heat or until golden and crisp.

## Stuffed Winter Squash

Served with chilled salad, this dish is ideal for a light supper.

**Ingredients:**
1 whole winter squash, about 1½–2 lb.
(700–900 g)
⅔ cup (100 g) okara
1 egg
½ cup minced mixed vegetables like carrot, string beans, celery and mushrooms
¼ teaspoon salt
1 tablespoon shoyu (soy sauce)
1 tablespoon sugar
2 tablespoons salad oil

**Method:**
1. Remove seeds of the winter squash, wash and pat dry.
2. In a bowl combine all the other ingredients and mix until blended. Pack this filling tightly into the cavity of the winter squash.
3. Bring steamer to high steam. Put stuffed winter squash in a bowl. Place in the steamer and steam for 30 minutes until the winter squash becomes soft.

Serves 4 as main dish, and 8 as warm hors d'oeuvres.

# Okara Cutlets

Serve with a sauce made with Worcestershire sauce and ketchup. Garnish with shredded cabbage.

**Ingredients:**
1¼ cups (185 g) packed okara
⅔ cup (100 g) flour
¼ teaspoon dry mustard
2 tablespoons soy sauce
¼ teaspoon sage
¼ teaspoon oregano
½ teaspoon salt
¼ cup (35 g) chopped onion
1 egg
1 cup (50 g) dry bread crumbs
Oil for frying

**Method:**
1. Mix all ingredients together except bread crumbs and oil. Shape into four cutlet-like shapes.
2. Coat with bread crumbs.
3. Fry cutlets in a little oil until brown on both sides and until the cutlets are no longer doughy inside.
4. Serve hot.

Makes 4 cutlets.

# Tofu Chicken Patties

**Ingredients:**
1¼ cups (300 g) tofu
10½ oz. (300 g) ground chicken meat, or any kind of ground meat
12 shiso leaves or nori
2 tablespoons arrowroot powder (or 3 tablespoons cornstarch)
Salt and pepper
Vegetable oil for frying
2 tablespoons grated ginger root
2 tablespoons mustard
Flour for dredging

**Method:**
1. Wrap tofu in a dry cloth to expel moisture, then crumble.
2. Combine tofu, ground chicken, and arrowroot in a bowl. Knead thoroughly until all the ingredients are well mixed. Season with salt and pepper. Make 12–16 patties. Dredge one side with flour.
3. Pour a little oil into a frying pan and heat.
4. Spread a shiso leaf on the floured side of the patty and fry in oil (shiso side first) until golden. Turn over and fry the other side.
5. Serve hot with shoyu (soy sauce), ginger and mustard.

**Note:**
Instead of spreading the shiso leaf onto the patty, you can drop tofu mixture by spoonfuls into the frying pan and sprinkle minced parsley or celery over the top of the patties. When the first side is done, turn the patties over and fry the other side until golden brown.

# Tofu Burgers

**Ingredients:**
1 cup (200 g) mashed tofu
1 cup cooked rice
½ cup (40 g) chopped onion
⅔ cup (100 g) all purpose flour
½ teaspoon basil
¼ teaspoon oregano
1 teaspoon salt
A dash of pepper
1 egg

**Method:**
1. Mix all ingredients together in a large bowl.
2. Shape into 6 burgers.
3. Fry burgers in a little salad oil until center is cooked and surface of the burger is browned.
4. Serve hot with ketchup, mustard and pickles.

Makes 6 burgers.

# Italian Tofu

Green salad and a glass of wine will complete the Italian feast!

**Ingredients:**
Tofu balls:
    1½ cups (300 g) mashed tofu
    ⅓ cup (45 g) chopped walnuts
    ½ small onion, chopped
    ⅓ cup (17 g) dry bread crumbs
    1 egg
    2 tablespoons chopped parsley
    ½ teaspoon salt
    Oil for deep-frying
Sauce:
    ¾ cup (375 ml) tomato sauce
    ¼ teaspoon oregano

**Method:**
Tofu balls:
1. Combine all the ingredients for tofu balls together with your hands until well combined. Set aside.
2. Heat oil for deep-frying.
3. Form 1½-inch balls (4 cm) with the tofu mixture. Fry balls until they are light brown in color and the center is no longer gummy. Drain on paper towels.
Sauce:
1. Mix sauce and oregano together in a saucepan. Heat.
2. Arrange tofu balls on plates. Pour sauce over the balls. Serve with pasta, if desired.

Makes 3 servings.

# Fine Chicken Fricassee with Tofu

If you are in a hurry omit blending. Cut boiled chicken and tofu and warm them in the sauce.

**Ingredients:**
1 whole chicken (1½ lb., 600 g)
10½ oz. (300 g) tofu, pressed with
  a light weight for 20 minutes
1 medium-sized carrot
1 stalk celery
3–4 sprigs parsley
1 medium-sized onion
1 cup (240 g) chopped and drained canned
  asparagus
1 cup (¼ l) milk
½ cup (⅛ l) white wine
4 cups (1 l) water
⅓ cup (30 g) bread crumbs
1 egg
2 teaspoons salt
A dash of pepper
3 bay leaves
Cream sauce:
  2 tablespoons butter
  3 tablespoons flour
  2 egg yolks, beaten

**Method:**
1. Place chicken in a large pot, add water, wine, carrot, onion, celery, parsley, bay leaves, salt and pepper. Cook over medium heat until chicken is tender. Skim broth occasionally.
2. Take chicken out of the broth and discard bones. Cut chicken meat and skin into small pieces.
3. Combine tofu and chicken pieces in a blender and blend until smooth. Pour into another bowl. Season with salt and pepper.
4. Add the bread crumbs and egg to the chicken mixture. Mix thoroughly. Season with salt and pepper.
5. Take carrot, onion and celery stalk out of the broth and chop coarsely. Set aside.
6. Strain broth. Measure 1½ cups (350 ml) broth and set aside for the cream sauce.
7. Bring remaining broth to a boil and drop the chicken/tofu mixture by spoonfuls into it. Let simmer for 15 minutes.
8. Cream sauce: Meanwhile, melt butter in a saucepan. Add flour and the 2 cups (½ l) reserved broth little by little to make a creamy sauce. Let simmer another 5 minutes over low heat, stirring constantly. Remove from heat, add egg yolks and mix until blended. Season to taste.
9. Add the cooked dumplings, vegetables and asparagus. Heat over low heat until all the ingredients are warm. Do not boil. Serve with rice.

# Lasagne

**Ingredients:**

Sauce:

    2 cups (½ l) tomato sauce

    1 cup (¼ l) water

    1 clove garlic, minced

    ½ teaspoon oregano

    1 teaspoon basil

    ⅛ teaspoon thyme

    1 teaspoon salt

    2 teaspoons sugar

    1 tablespoon salad oil

Filling:

    2 eggs

    1 lb. (450 g) tofu

    ½ teaspoon salt

    6 tablespoons grated Parmesan cheese

    ¼ cup minced parsley

Lasagne:

    ¾ lb. (330 g) lasagne noodles, cooked and drained

    ½ lb. (225 g) Mozzarella cheese, grated

**Method:**

1. Sauce: Combine all sauce ingredients in a saucepan and simmer for about 1 hour. While sauce is simmering, prepare the filling.
2. Filling: Mix together all filling ingredients. Filling will be lumpy.
3. Lasagne: Oil a baking dish 7½ × 11½ inches (19 × 29 cm). Put one layer of lasagne noodles in the bottom of the dish. Pour ⅓ of the sauce on top of the noodles.
4. Spread ½ of the tofu mixture on top of the sauce. Again, put down a layer of noodles, layer of sauce and the remaining tofu-cheese mixture.
5. Use the remaining noodles and cover with sauce. Cover baking dish with foil and bake at 325°F. (160°C.) for about 30 minutes.
6. Remove foil, and sprinkle top of lasagne with the shredded Mozzarella cheese.
7. Bake for about another 15 minutes, or until cheese is bubbly. Cut into squares, and serve hot.

Makes 6 servings.

# Gratin of Tofu, Eggplants and Tomatoes

Tomato and cheese go very well with tofu. You can serve this dish with Worcestershire sauce for a change.

**Ingredients:**

1 lb. and 5 oz. (about 600 g) tofu

3 large ripe tomatoes

8 small or 3 large Japanese eggplants

⅓ cup (40 g) grated Parmesan cheese

2 tablespoons olive oil

1 teaspoon salt

**Method:**

1. Wrap tofu in 2 large cloths and let stand for 20 minutes, until it becomes firm. Then cut into slices about ⅓-inch (8 mm) thick. Spread the slices on a new cloth to expel moisture.
2. Cut eggplants and tomatoes into slices the same thickness as the tofu. Deep-fry eggplant for a short time. Drain on a paper towels.
3. Arrange tofu, deep-fried eggplant and tomatoes in layers so that all the slices can be seen. Sprinkle salt olive oil, then Parmesan cheese over all. Bake at 375°F. (190°C.) for 30 minutes, or until the top is browned.

Serves 4–6.

# Tofu Flambé

Serve this dish under candle light in a cozy room on a cold winter night.

**Ingredients:**
1¼ cups (300 g) tofu
½ cup (70 g) flour
3 tablespoons minced onion
1 cup (¼ l) fresh cream
½ cup (⅛ l) brandy
1 teaspoon salt
A pinch of salt
1 tablespoon lemon juice
2 tablespoons butter

**Method:**
1. Press tofu with a heavy weight for 20 minutes.
2. Cut tofu horizontally into 4 slices. Sprinkle with lemon. Dust with flour. Sauté on both sides until golden brown. Keep warm.
3. Melt butter in a skillet. Fry onion for 1 minute. Add cream and bring to a boil. Season with pepper and add some more salt, if necessary.
4. Place tofu into the warm sauce.
5. Pour brandy into a large metal ladel, hold it in the hot sauce to warm it up, then ignite. Pour flaming brandy over the tofu. Stir sauce gently to burn off all the alcohol. Serve immediately after the flame goes out.

# Deep-Fried Tofu Sandwich ★

Serve immediately to enjoy a crisp crust.

**Ingredients:**
1 lb. and 5 oz. (600 g) tofu
4 small slices of ham
4 small slices of cheese
½ cup ground pork or beef
1 teaspoon grated ginger root
¼ teaspoon salt
½ cup flaked tuna
1 tablespoon mayonnaise
4 thin slices of onion
½ cup (65 g) arrowroot powder or corn-starch
Vegetable oil for deep-frying
Salt and lemon juice as condiment

**Method:**
1. Cut tofu into 12 slices. Spread them on paper towels to expel as much moisture as possible. Then cut a slit in the middle of each tofu slice.
2. Combine ground meat, ginger and salt. Mix until blended. In another bowl blend tuna and mayonnaise.
3. Fill 4 tofu slices 4 with ham/cheese, and the remaining 4 ground meat or tuna/onion stuffing. Coat tofu sandwich thoroughly with arrowroot.
4. Heat oil. Deep-fry tofu sandwich quickly over high heat.
5. Serve immediately with salt and lemon juice.

Serves 4.

# Steamed Tofu Custard with Asparagus Tips

Serve this delicate dish instead of soup.

**Ingredients:**
1½ cups (300 g) tofu
4 egg whites
About 30 tips and parts of canned white
    asparagus, drained (save liquid)
1 cup (¼ l) milk
½ teaspoon salt
For the center decoration (scrambled eggs):
    4 egg yolks and 1 whole egg
    ¼ teaspoon salt
    A little pepper
    2 tablespoons vegetable oil
    5 stalks green asparagus
For the sauce:
    1 cup (¼ l) liquid from the canned
        asparagus
    ½ instant bouillon cube
    1 tablespoon cornstarch

**Method:**
1. Purée tofu in a blender until smooth.
2. In a bowl, gently stir egg whites with a fork.
3. Combine with tofu, milk and salt. Mix gently. Set aside.
4. Cover the bottom of a deep serving bowl with asparagus. Pour tofu mixture through a strainer over the asparagus.
5. Bring steamer to a full boil, then reduce heat to low. Set the bowl into the steamer and steam for 12–15 minutes.
6. While tofu custard is steaming, make scrambled eggs. (Beat yolks and egg with salt and pepper and fry in oil.) Set aside.
7. Cut green asparagus into 1-inch (3 cm) pieces. Fry in a little oil. Do not overcook. The asparagus has to retain its green color and stay crisp. Sprinkle with a pinch of salt.
8. In a saucepan bring asparagus liquid to a boil. Add bouillon cube. Correct seasoning, if necessary. Dissolve cornstarch in a little water and add to the soup. Cook for another minute, stirring constantly, until thickened.
9. Take the bowl of tofu custard out of the steamer. Pour sauce over the tofu custard and place green asparagus and scrambled egg in the center. Serve by scooping out the custard with a spoon into an individual bowl.

# Vegetable Soufflé

Peas are used here, but any leftover cooked vegetable would be wonderful in this hearty soufflé.

**Ingredients:**
1 onion, chopped
1½ cups (200 g) sliced mushrooms
1 tablespoon salad oil
3 tablespoons chopped parsley
1 tablespoon white wine (optional)
½ teaspoon salt
1⅓ cups (300 g) mashed tofu
½ cup (70 g) wheat germ
1 cup (150 g) cooked, drained green peas
1 cup (¼ l) milk
1 tablespoon cornstarch
3 egg yolks
3 egg whites

**Method:**
1. Sauté onions and mushrooms in oil until onions are transparent. Take off heat.
2. Add parsley, wine, salt, mashed tofu, wheat germ and peas to the sautéd vegetables. Set aside.
3. In a saucepan, mix milk and cornstarch together. Cook and stir constantly over low heat until mixture becomes thick.
4. Lightly beat 3 egg yolks in a small bowl. Add a little hot milk mixture to the egg yolks. Combine all of the milk mixture to egg yolks and stir until blended.
5. Return egg yolk-milk mixture to the saucepan and cook over low heat, stirring constantly, until thickened. Don't boil!
6. Gently stir sauce into the tofu mixture.
7. In another bowl, whip egg whites until stiff.
8. Fold tofu mixture into the egg whites.
9. Gently spoon soufflé into a straight sided baking dish or into individual cups that have been greased and dusted with wheat germ.
10. Bake at 350°F. (180°C.) for about 45 minutes or until soufflé is set and lightly browned.
11. Serve soufflé immediately.

Makes 6 servings.

# Tofu Crabmeat Gratin

Delicate dish for a fastidious palate.

**Ingredients:**
10½ oz. (300 g) tofu
3 tablespoons butter
⅓ cup (80 g) sliced onion
⅓ cup (80 g) sliced celery
3 oz. (80 g) carrot, cut into matchsticks
½ teaspoon salt
A dash of pepper
3 tablespoons butter
2 tablespoons flour
1 tablespoon + 1 teaspoon (20 ml) brandy
1 cup (¼ l) fish stock
1 cup (¼ l) milk
1 cup (200 g) shredded cooked crabmeat
1 stick crabmeat
3 tablespoons minced parsley
1 tablespoon minced fresh tarragon

**Method:**
1. Wrap tofu in a cloth and let stand for 15 minutes. Dice.
2. Fry onion, celery and carrot with butter in a pan until translucent and soft, but not mushy. Season with salt and pepper.
3. In another frying pan melt another 3 tablespoons butter, add flour and cook for 2 minutes, stirring constantly to avoid burning.
4. Add brandy and continue cooking over low heat.
5. Add fish stock and milk and cook for 5 minutes until smooth, stirring constantly.
6. Add diced tofu, crabmeat, parsley and tarragon. Simmer another 2 minutes. Correct seasoning.
7. Pour into 4 individual shallow dishes. Cut crabmeat stick into 4 and place each pieces in the center of the dish as a decoration. If available you can use crab shells, cooked and cleaned, to give a professional air. Broil until the top is browned.
8. Serve hot.

Serves 4.

# Steamed Tofu Sandwich

A delightful combination of mild tofu and spicy filling. Sauce plays an important role, too.

**Ingredients:**
1 lb. + 6 oz. (600 g) tofu
½ lb. (225 g) ground pork or chicken
2 tablespoons minced onion
2 tablespoons fresh green peppercorns, chopped
1 tablespoon cornstarch
1 tablespoon cornstarch for dredging tofu
½ teaspoon salt for filling
½ teaspoon salt for tofu
For mustard sauce:
  ½ cup (120 ml) mayonnaise
  2 tablespoons hot mustard
  1 tablespoon Worcestershire sauce
  2 tablespoons sherry
  1 teaspoon curry powder
  3 tablespoons milk

**Method:**
1. Cut tofu into 8 slices about ½-inch (13 mm) thick. Place them on a large dish cloth, cover with another dish cloth and let stand for 15 minutes. Change cloths once or twice if necessary to absorb as much moisture as possible. Then sprinkle salt evenly over tofu slices. (If you cut out circles as shown in the picture, do not throw away leftover chunks but save to mix then into the meat filling.)
2. In a bowl combine ground meat, onion, green peppercorns, cornstarch and left-over tofu chunks. Mix until blended. Season with ½ teaspoon salt. Divide into 4 portions.
3. Dredge one side of the tofu slices with cornstarch. Make into sandwiches starched side in.
4. Bring a steamer to full boil. Reduce heat, place tofu sandwiches into the steamer and steam over medium heat for 12 minutes or until the meat filling is done.
5. Meanwhile in a bowl, blend all the ingredients for the sauce. Serve the hot tofu sandwiches with the mustard sauce.

# Artichoke Hearts with Tofu Sesame Sauce

This sauce goes well with any cooked vegetable.

**Ingredients:**
16 artichoke hearts (canned or freshly boiled), drained
½ cup (170 g) mashed tofu
3 tablespoons ground sesame seeds
1 teaspoon salt
½ teaspoon sugar
1 tablespoon sesame oil
2 tablespoon lemon juice or vinegar

**Method:**
1. Squeeze tofu to remove excess liquid.
2. In a blender combine all ingredients except artichoke hearts and blend until smooth. Stop the blender from time to time and scrape the wall with a rubber spatula.
3. Cut artichoke hearts in chunks or slices and mix with the sauce.

**Variation:**
Add 3 hard boiled egg yolks to the sauce, mash until smooth, and pipe it onto the artichoke hearts. Serve them as hors d'oeuvre.

**Note:**
This recipe makes about ½ cup sauce. If the blender is large, it is easier to take double the amount.

## Tofu Hot Pot

A good way to reshuffle the contents of
your refrigerator.

**Ingredients:**
10 oz. (300 g) tofu
1 medium-sized onion
1 carrot
1 stalk celery
2–3 cabbage leaves
4 small turnips
Soup stock
Salt and pepper
4 eggs

**Method:**
1. Clean and peel onion, carrot, turnips and
   cut into bite-sized pieces. Chop celery
   and cabbage.
2. Cook onion, carrot and celery in the
   soup stock until soft. Add cabbage and
   turnips and cook another 5 minutes. Do
   not overcook. The vegetables should remain crisp.
3. Season with salt and pepper.
4. Cut tofu into bite-sized pieces. Add to
   the other vegetables. Cook over medium
   heat until tofu is warm.
5. Drop eggs gently onto the vegetables.
   Cook until egg white is set.
6. Divide into 4 individual soup bowls.
   Serve hot with garlic toast.

Serves 4.

## Tofu in Hot Soup, Korean Style

**Ingredients:**
2 lb. (500 g) tofu
2 lb. (500 g) kimchi of Chinese cabbage
1 cup (¼ l) soup stock or water
3 tablespoons shoyu (soy sauce)
1 clove garlic, grated
½ teaspoon sugar
1 tablespoon sesame oil
1 tablespoon ground red pepper

**Method:**
1. Cut tofu and cabbage kimchi in bite-
   sized pieces.
2. Combine rest of the ingredients in a pot
   and bring to a boil.
3. Add tofu and kimchi and cook for 5
   minutes.

You may reduce the amount of red pepper.
Season with salt, if necessary.

# Broiled Tofu with Miso Sauce

Miso-sesame combination gives a Japanese touch to this dish.

**Ingredients:**
1 lb. (450 g) tofu
Sesame oil for frying
Miso sauce:
  ½ cup (125 g) miso★
  ¼ cup (50 g) sugar
  ¼ cup (60 ml) sake or sherry
  2 tablespoons grated ginger root
  1 tablespoon ground sesame seeds

**Method:**
1. Cut tofu into pieces about ½ inch (1.3 cm) thick. Wrap in a dry cloth to expel moisture.
2. Fry tofu on both sides until brown.
3. In a saucepan combine all ingredients for the sauce and cook over low heat for about 30 minutes, stirring constantly to avoid sticking. Add water or sake, if the sauce is too thick.
4. Arrange fried tofu in a casserole so that the bottom of the casserole is covered. Spread with miso sauce, sprinkle with sesame seeds and bake in a hot oven until the sauce begins to bubble. Serve hot.

Serves 4.

★ Miso, or fermented soybean paste, is available in Oriental food stores. Reduce the amount of miso if it is too salty.

# Tofu with Meat Sauce

Vary the sauce by substituting salt for the miso or shoyu, adding cayenne pepper, tomato paste or anchovy paste.

**Ingredients:**
1 lb. and 5 oz. (600 g) tofu
2 tablespoons minced onion
1 tablespoon minced garlic
3 tablespoons vegetable oil
1 cup (200 g) lean ground pork or beef
1 teaspoon salt
½ teaspoon pepper
½ cup (¼ l) soup stock or water
3 tablespoons sour cream
2 tablespoons cornstarch, dissolved in
  2 tablespoons water

**Method:**
1. In a frypan heat oil. Fry garlic and onion for a few minutes over medium heat. Add ground meat and brown. Season with salt and pepper. Add water and sour cream and bring back to boil. Add cornstarch and cook until thickened.
2. In a pan bring 1 cup (¼ l) of water together with 2 teaspoons of salt to a boil. Cook tofu in it for 3 minutes. Drain and keep warm.
3. Cut tofu into 4 portions. Pour sauce over it and serve hot.

Serves 4.

# Fried Tofu with Green Onion

Fry over very low heat to get the bright yellow color of the egg coating. Do not let them burn.

**Ingredients:**
1 lb. (450 g) tofu
2 eggs
½ cup shredded red chili pepper
½ cup green spring onion, cut into thin
   strips
1 tablespoon flour
Salt
For the sauce:
   1 cup (¼ l) soup stock
   ¼ cup (60 ml) shoyu (soy sauce)
   ¼ cup (60 g) sugar
   1 teaspoon crushed garlic
   2 teaspoons grated ginger root
   ½ teaspoon powdered red pepper
   ½ pear or apple, grated

**Method:**
1. Cut tofu into 8 oblong slices and wrap in dry cloth to expel moisture.
2. Sprinkle a little salt over tofu slices. Place a few strips of spring onion and red chili pepper onto a tofu slice. Set aside.
3. Beat egg and flour thoroughly. Dip tofu slice carefully into the beaten egg, then fry on a greased griddle (onion side down) over low heat until the egg coating is firm. Turn over and fry the other side.
4. In a saucepan combine soup stock, shoyu and sugar. Bring to a boil. Take off heat and add the other ingredients and spices.
5. Divide the sauce in 4 individual bowls. Serve tofu with the sauce.

★ You can substitute young celery leaves, watercress or minced parsley for spring onion.

Serves 2.

# Chilled Tofu with Green Sauce

Very simple and healthy, this dish can be served as hors d'oeuvre, salad or snack.

**Ingredients:**
1 lb. (450 g) tofu
½ cup (¼ l) dry white wine
2 teaspoons salt
1 cup minced fresh herbs (parsley, mint,
   oregano, dill, chives, etc.)
1 tablespoon minced pickles
1 tablespoon minced green olives
2 tablespoons salad oil
2 tablespoons vinegar
½ teaspoon salt
¼ teaspoon pepper
Several slices of stuffed olives as garnish

**Method:**
1. In a saucepan bring 1 cup (¼ l) water to a boil. Add salt. Place tofu carefully into the pan and cook covered for 2 minutes. Drain.
2. Slide tofu slice into a bowl. Pour wine over it. Cover with a clear wrap and chill in the refrigerator.
3. Pat chilled tofu with kitchen towel. Place on a serving plate and cut into slices about ⅓ inch (8 mm) thick.
4. In a bowl combine all the ingredients for sauce and mix thoroughly. Pour this sauce over the tofu and garnish with olive slices.

Serves 4 as hors d'oeuvre.

## Hot Okara Wrapped in Lettuce Leaves

Vary spices according to your imagination. An effective way to use up leftover vegetables.

**Ingredients:**
½ cup minced shiitake (black Japanese mushrooms)
½ cup minced carrot
½ cup minced celery
½ minced onion
½ cup minced pine nuts or walnuts
4 tablespoons sesame oil
2–2½ cups (300 g) okara
3 tablespoons shoyu (soy sauce)
3 tablespoons sake
1 tablespoon chili pepper powder (reduce the amount according to your taste)
8–12 lettuce leaves

**Method:**
1. Heat sesame oil in a frying pan. Sauté vegetables and pine nuts for 5 minutes.
2. Add okara and continue to sauté.
3. Add seasonings and sauté another 5 minutes. Remove from heat.
4. Wash and drain lettuce leaves. Pat dry with kitchen cloth. Serve lettuce leaves on a platter accompanied by the okara vegetables.
5. To eat, take 2 tablespoonfuls of okara on a lettuce leaf and wrap up.

Serves 4–6.

## Roasted Chicken with Okara Stuffing

In this dish it is the spicy stuffing rather than the chicken that is the main attraction.

**Ingredients:**
1 whole chicken, about 2 lb. (900 g)
2 teaspoons salt
1 teaspoon sugar
½ teaspoon pepper
2 teaspoons paprika
1 cup (140 g) okara
1 egg
3 tablespoons each of minced parsley, celery, onion
1 teaspoon thyme
½ teaspoon pepper
A pinch each of powdered clove and cardamom
½ teaspoon salt
2 tablespoons brandy

**Method:**
1. Combine 2 teaspoons salt, sugar and paprika. Rub chicken inside and outside with it. Set aside.
2. Combine all the other ingredients, (except chicken) and mix until blended. Then stuff chicken with it. Close the opening with kitchen twine or toothpicks. Brush with oil.
3. Roast chicken in a moderate oven for about 1 hour. Or until drumstick can easily be moved back and forth.

Serves 4–6.

# Agé Risotto

Agé gives rich taste to this simple rice dish. You can substitute salmon with almost any other fish.

**Ingredients:**
1½ cups (300 g) rice
2¼ cups (560–600 ml) water
2 tablespoons vegetable oil
½ cup (65 g) minced onion
4 pieces agé (about 2 × 4 inches, 5 × 10 cm)
½ lb. (225 g) salmon fillet
1 cup (200 g) green peas
1 cup (150 g) sliced mushrooms
1 teaspoon salt
A dash of pepper

**Method:**
1. Wash rice and drain in a colander for at least 30 minutes.
2. In a saucepan sauté onion in oil. Add rice and sauté another 5 minutes, or until rice becomes translucent.
3. Add water, agé, salmon, peas and mushrooms, season with salt and pepper. Bring to a boil. Cook over high heat for 5 minutes. Reduce heat to low and cook covered for 15 minutes or until rice is done.

Serves 4.

# Grilled Agé

Very simple and easy to make. Makes an excellent hors d'oeuvre.

**Ingredients:**
4 pieces agé, about 2 × 4 inches (5 × 10 cm) each
2 tablespoons red miso
1 tablespoon sugar
2 tablespoons minced green onion

**Method:**
1. Cut a slit through the long side of the agé pieces. Pull them apart with your fingers to make a pouch with wide openings (see page 127). Set aside.
2. In a small bowl combine miso, sugar and green onion. Mix until blended. Divide into 4 portions.
3. With a knife spread miso evenly inside the agé pouches.
4. Grill or sauté filled agé pouches on both sides until brown and crisp.
5. Cut in bite-sized pieces and serve.

# Surprise Agé Pouches

An elegant way to use up leftover vegetables.

**Ingredients:**
8 pieces agé, about 1½ × 5 inches
    (4 × 12.5 cm)
½ carrot, cut into matchsticks
½ stalk celery, cut into matchsticks
A handful spinach leaves, parboiled
2 strips bacon, chopped
4 eggs
2 potatoes, grated and drained
8 gingko nuts, parboiled and peeled
String or toothpicks to close the pouches
1½ cups (375 ml) water
1 bouillon cube

**Method:**
1. Cut agé in half and pull them apart to
   make 16 pouches  (see page 127).
2. Fill 4 of the pouches with carrots and
   celery, the next 4 with spinach and
   bacon. Stuff 4 with potato and gingko
   nuts. Drop an egg into each of the last 4
   pouches. Tie the opening with a string
   or fasten it with a toothpick.
3. In a shallow saucepan or skillet combine
   water and bouillon cube. Bring to a boil.
   Place in a single layer the stuffed agé
   pouches into the broth. Cook over
   medium heat for 10 minutes.
4. Arrange cooked pouches on a large serving dish. Serve with cooked rice.

Serves 4.

**Note:**
If kampyo is available, tie the pouches with
it, as shown in the picture. Wash kampyo
under running water throughly before using.

# Steamed Yuba Rolls

Vary the filling (shrimp, chopped nuts, chicken, etc.) and enjoy different taste and texture.

**Ingredients:**
8 sheets dried yuba (5 × 4 inches,
   12.5 × 10 cm)
1½ cups (300 g) tofu
½ lb. (200 g) ground pork
½ cup minced shiitake★ or mushroom
3 tablespoons minced green onion
1 tablespoon grated ginger root
½ teaspoon salt
1 teaspoon shoyu (soy sauce)
½ teaspoon sugar

**Method:**
1. Reconstitute yuba (page 124). Set aside.
2. Wrap tofu in a dry cloth and let stand for 20 minutes. Crumble.
3. Combine all the ingredients in a bowl and knead thoroughly with your hands until smooth.
4. Divide tofu mixture into 8 portions and spread evenly on the yuba sheets, leaving ¼ inch (6 mm) edge on one side. Set aside.
5. Dissolve cornstarch in a little water and brush the free edge with it. Tightly roll the yuba toward free edge.
6. Bring steamer to full steam. Place yuba rolls into the steamer seam-side down and steam over high heat for 20 minutes.
7. Cut the rolls in half and serve hot with shoyu and mustard.

★ Shiitake: Black Japanese mushrooms, usually sold dried in Oriental food stores. To reconstitute, soak them in luke warm water for 30 minutes.

# Stuffed Fried Yuba Rolls

Crisp treat as hors d'oeuvre or snack. Vary the filling to suprise your friends.

**Ingredients:**
4 sheets of fresh or reconstituted yuba
   (about 4 × 5 inches, 10 × 12.5 cm)
For filling:
   Boiled ginkgo nuts, ground meat with minced onions, grated cheese, cooked minced sausages, bacon and tomatoes, etc.
Salt
Salad oil for deep-frying
1 egg white, well beaten

**Method:**
1. Cut yuba sheets into halves.
2. Place 1 tablespoonful of different fillings onto the center of yuba. Fold it like an envelope and roll into a slim stick. Moisten roll flap with egg white. Set aside with the seam-side down. Fill and wrap remaining yuba sheets.
3. Deep-fry yuba rolls until crisp. Do not burn.
4. Sprinkle with a little salt and serve hot.

# Herb Dressing

Wonderful on a salad, or as a dip for vegetables.

**Ingredients:**
¾ cup (175 ml) Tofu Mayonnaise
   (page 74)
¾ cup (175 ml) yogurt
1 cup (225 g) mashed tofu
½ teaspoon minced dill weed
½ teaspoon salt
A dash of pepper
1 tablespoon minced parsley
1 tablespoon minced onion

**Method:**
1. Combine first 6 ingredients together in a blender until smooth.
2. By hand, stir in the parsley and onion. Pour into a serving dish.
3. Chill until serving time.

Makes about 2½ cups.

# Tofu Cottage Cheese

Scoops of this tofu treat served in a fresh pineapple shell makes any lunch a special event!

**Ingredients:**
1⅓ cups (250 g) drained and pressed tofu
2–3 tablespoons yogurt or sour cream
½ teaspoon salt

**Method:**
1. Using a table knife or fork, mix all ingredients together until texture resembles ordinary cottage cheese.
2. Chill mixture before serving for best flavor.

Makes 1⅓ cups.

# Tofu Mayonnaise

One of the classics in America's tofu cuisine.

**Ingredients:**
1 cup (200 g) mashed tofu
½ cup (1/8 l) salad oil
3 tablespoons vinegar
¼ teaspoon dry mustard
½ teaspoon salt

**Method:**
1. Put all ingredients in a blender and purée until smooth.
2. Use as you would regular mayonnaise.
3. Store tofu mayonnaise in a covered jar in the refrigerator. Keeps well for about 2 weeks.

Makes about 1¾ cups.

# Tofu Cream Cheese    

Use Tofu Cream Cheese as you would regular cream cheese, but with a clear conscience —Only 200 fat calories in the whole recipe. And it is unsaturated!

**Ingredients:**
1½ cups (300 g) drained and pressed tofu
2 tablespoons salad oil
¼ teaspoon salt (or to taste)

**Method:**
1. Put all ingredients in a blender and mix until smooth. Since most of the water has been pressed out of the tofu you may have to stop the blender, push ingredients to the center of the blender jar with a rubber spatula and blend again.
2. For best flavor, serve chilled.

Makes about 1½ cups.

# Cooked Salad with Tofu

**Ingredients:**
1 lb. (450 g) tofu
2 zucchinis
1 small-sized eggplant
2 stalks celery
A bunch of string beans
2 medium-sized onions
2 large or 4 medium-sized green peppers
For broth:
  2 cups (½ l) water
  2 bouillon cubes
  1 teaspoon salt
  1 teaspoon pepper
  3 bay leaves
For marinade:
  ½ cup (120 ml) salad oil
  ½ cup (120 ml) vinegar
  1 tablespoon sugar
For garnish:
  3 tablespoons minced parsley

**Method:**
1. Place tofu on a plate, sprinkle with 1 tea-spoon salt and steam in a steamer over high heat for 10 minutes. Take out and let cool on a mesh or bamboo mat.
2. Cut vegetables in large chunks.
3. In a large pot, bring ingredients for broth to a boil. Cook vegetables in it for 10 minutes.
4. Turn off heat and add ingredients for marinade. Mix carefully.
5. Cut tofu in cubes and add to the vege-tables. Chill.
6. Spoon tofu and vegetables out of broth and arrange on serving plate.
7. Before serving, sprinkle with parsley.

Serves 8.

# Deviled Tofu Salad

Variations of this salad are found in most of America's Soy Delis—a classic in American tofu cuisine.

**Ingredients:**
2 tablespoons tofu mayonnaise (see page 74)

2 teaspoons vinegar
¼ teaspoon dry mustard
½ teaspoon salt
¼ teaspoon garlic powder
¼ teaspoon turmeric
1¾ cups (400 g) tofu (drained and pressed)

**Method:**
1. Mix all ingredients except tofu into a bowl.
2. Add tofu, and mix with a spatula to make small "chunks." Chill.
3. Serve on a lettuce leaf, or use as a sand-wich filling.

Makes 3 generous servings.

# Tofu Tuna Salad in Tomato Aspic Ring

**Ingredients:**
For the aspic:
  4½ tablespoons (40 g) powdered gelatin
  1 cup (¼ l) fish broth
  1 cup (¼ l) tomato juice
  ½ cup (⅛ l) dry white wine
  1 tablespoon vinegar
  1 tablespoon paprika powder
For salad:
  10 oz. (300 g) tofu
  1 can (6 oz., 180 g) of white tuna, drained
  Juice of 1 lemon
  1 tablespoon minced capers
  2 tablespoons minced pickled cucumbers
  2 tablespoons minced onion
  1 tablespoon hot mustard
  2 tablespoons mayonnaise
  Salt and pepper
For garnish:
  Parsley

**Method:**
1. Wrap tofu in a large cloth and press for 10 minutes. Dice half of it into ⅕-inch (5 mm) cubes. Set aside.
2. Soak gelatin in ¼ cup broth.
3. In a saucepan combine the rest of the broth, tomato juice and wine. Bring to a boil. Remove from heat.
4. Add soaked gelatin and stir until dis-solved.

5. Add vinegar and paprika. Season with salt and pepper to taste. Let cool.
6. Rinse ring mold with cold water. Pour a little gelatin solution into the mold, just enough to cover the bottom. Sprinkle with a handful of tofu cubes. Set in the refrigerator to chill.
7. Meanwhile, chill the rest of the gelatin over ice solution water. When the gelatin begins to thicken, add the rest of the tofu cubes and mix gently. Pour the mixture into the ring mold and chill in the refrigerator.
8. While the aspic is becoming firm, mash the other half of the tofu with a fork. Add tuna and crumble to flakes. Add lemon juice, capers, pickles, onion, mustard and mayonnaise. Mix thoroughly. Season with salt and pepper to taste.
9. When the aspic is set, turn it onto a serving plate. Fill the center with tuna salad. Garnish with parsley.

## Tofu Seafood Salad

**Ingredients:**
10 oz. (300 g) tofu
3 tablespoons shoyu (soy sauce)
10 oz. (300 g) shrimp, fresh or frozen
10 oz. (300 g) scallops, fresh or frozen
5 oz. (150 g) octopus, cooked
3½ oz. (100 g) fresh string beans
4 stalks watercress
For dressing:
   ¼ cup minced fresh dill
   ¼ cup (250 ml) vinegar
   ¼ cup (250 ml) salad oil
   ½ teaspoon salt
   ½ teaspoon sugar
   A dash of white pepper

**Method:**
1. Simmer tofu in salted water for 5 minutes. Drain. Place on a plate and pour shoyu over it, wrap airtight and chill in the refrigerator for at least 2 hours.
2. Clean shrimp, discard shells and devein. Cook in salted water for 2 minutes until the color changes to bright pink.
3. Parboil scallops by adding them to the boiling shrimp. Drain.

4. Cut octopus into bite-sized pieces. Chill seafood.
5. Meanwhile, wash string beans. Cut into 1-inch (2.5 cm) pieces. Parboil in salted water, then cool under cold running water to keep the color. Drain and set aside.
6. Combine all the ingredients for dressing in a bowl.
7. Marinate seafood and string beans in the dressing for a short time. Then take them out of the marinade and arrange in a large salad bowl.
8. Cut tofu into bite-sized pieces and place on the seafood. Pour marinade over, garnish with watercress and serve.

Serves 8.

## Tofu Wakamé Salad

**Ingredients:**
10 oz. (300 g) tofu
2 oz. (60 g) cucumber
Salt
7 oz. (200 g) wakamé (about 2 cups), cleaned, soaked in water until soft and chopped
For dressing:
   3 tablespoons shoyu (soy sauce)
   3 tablespoons vinegar
   3 tablespoons sesame oil
   2 tablespoons salad oil
   1 teaspoon sugar
   2 tablespoons ground sesame seeds
   ½ teaspoon cayenne pepper
   2 teaspoons mustard

**Method:**
1. Wrap tofu in a cloth and let stand for 15 minutes. Then cut into bite-sized pieces.
2. Slice cucumber very thinly, sprinkle with a little salt and wait till water beads. Then squeeze with both hands to expel water.
3. Arrange tofu, cucumber and wakamé on a plate.
4. Beat all the ingredients for dressing in a bowl. Pour over salad just before serving.

PART II

82

84

86

88

90

92

96

100

102

104

106

108

112

# Tofu White Chocolate Cream

An exquisite holiday dessert.

**Ingredients:**
½ cup (170 g) mashed tofu
½ cup (⅛ l) milk
2¼ teaspoons (5 g) powdered gelatin, dissolved in 1 tablespoon water
3½ oz. (100 g) white chocolate
2 tablespoons honey (adjust the amount according to the sweetness of the chocolate used)
A pinch of cardamom, mace and cinnamon
Sliced, toasted almonds as garnish

**Method:**
1. Wrap tofu in a cloth and let stand for 15 minutes. Then blend until smooth. Set aside.
2. Warm milk and dissolve gelatin in it. Do not let boil. Set aside.
3. In a double boiler, melt chocolate.
4. Add milk, chocolate, honey and spices to the tofu purée and blend again. Let cool.
5. Spoon into individual glasses and chill. Before serving garnish with toasted almond slices.

Makes 2 generous or 4 small portions.

# Banana Pudding Pie

Garnish with fresh banana slices and swirls of Tofu Whip (page 117).

**Ingredients:**
1 tablespoon (9 g) gelatin
6 tablespoons water
1⅓ cups (280 g) mashed tofu
1 egg
¼ cup (45 g) sugar
Juice of 1 lemon
⅛ teaspoon salt
2 large bananas
1 crumb crust pie shell (page 115)

**Method:**
1. In a small saucepan soak gelatin in 3 tablespoons water for 5 minutes. Add 3 more tablespoons of water. Melt the gelatin over low heat, until gelatin is completely dissolved. Do not boil!
2. Mix remaining 6 ingredients together in a blender until smooth. Add melted gelatin, and blend until well mixed.
3. Pour filling into crumb crust. Chill for at least 4 hours, or overnight.
4. Garnish as desired, or as suggested above.

Makes one 9-inch (23 cm) pie.

# Tofu Mango Dessert

Makes a thrilling finish for your meal.

**Ingredients:**
1 cup (200 g) mashed tofu
2 mangos (about 1 lb., 450 g)
Juice of 1 lemon
⅔ cup (200 ml) heavy cream
1 egg yolk
3 tablespoons (27 g) powdered gelatin
1 cup (¼ l) water
⅔ cup (120 g) sugar
For garnish:
   1 mango

**Method:**
1. Peel and dice mangos. Combine mango, tofu and egg yolk in a blender. Blend until smooth. Set aside.
2. Soak gelatin in 3 tablespoons cold water.
3. In a saucepan, combine water and sugar. Heat until sugar is dissolved. Do not boil.
4. Pour into a bowl. Add lemon juice, tofu-mango mixture and stir until blended. Chill.
5. Meanwhile, whip cream. When the gelatin mixture begins to thicken, fold in whipped cream.
6. Rinse 6 small molds (or a quart mold) with cold water. Fill with the mango cream. Chill.
7. To serve, decorate with mango slices.

Serves 6.

**Note:**
If mango is not available you can substitute pineapple. Use 1 cup crushed canned pineapple and 1 cup (¼ l) pineapple juice instead of mango, lemon and the water.

# Tofu Lemon Dessert

Fluffy and refreshing. A perfect dessert after a spicy dish.

**Ingredients:**
1 lemon
1 cup (200 g) mashed tofu
3 tablespoons (27 g) powdered gelatin, soaked in 3 tablespoons cold water
¾ cup (150 g) sugar
1¼ cups (310 ml) water
Juice of 1½ lemons
1 egg white
For garnish:
   Raspberry sauce

**Method:**
1. Chill 6 dessert molds, each of which holds ½ cup (125 ml) liquid, in a freezer.
2. Peel lemon. Cut very thin slices. Set aside.
3. Purée tofu in a blender until smooth.
4. In a saucepan combine water and sugar. Heat until sugar is dissolved. Add soaked gelatin and dissolve over low heat. Do not boil.
5. Add lemon juice and mix. Let cool.
6. Meanwhile beat egg white until stiff.
7. To coat the mold, fill it with cooled gelatin to the brim. Let stand for a while in a refrigerator until a film of gelatin has coated the wall and the bottom of the mold. Pour gelatin back to the saucepan. Place a slice of lemon into the bottom of mold. Repeat process with the other molds.
8. Combine tofu and the remaining gelatin in a bowl. Mix well. Chill to the consistency of egg white.
9. Fold in beaten egg white. Pour the mixture into the gelatin coated molds. Chill in refrigerator.
10. To serve set the molds into warm water for a short time. Turn over onto a plate. Decorate with raspberry sauce.

Serves 6.

**Raspberry Sauce:**
Purée 1⅔ cups (200 g) ripe raspberries. Add ½ cup (100 g) sugar and ¼ cup (60 ml) cointreau. Mix well until sugar is dissolved. Strain.

Makes 2 cups (240 g) sauce.

# Vanilla Coffee Bavarian Cream

A round coffee filling in the center of vanilla pudding will be a pleasant surprise for your guests.

## Ingredients:

1¼ cups (300 g, 10 oz.) tofu
3 tablespoons (27 g) powdered gelatin
4 egg yolks
1 cup (180 g) sugar
2 cups (½ l) milk
½ teaspoon vanilla extract
½ cup + ⅓ cup (200 ml) heavy cream
1 tablespoon instant coffee

## Method:

1. Wrap tofu in a cloth and let stand for 30 minutes.
2. Soak gelatin in ¼ cup (60 ml) cold water. Set aside.
3. Purée tofu in a blender until smooth. Set aside.
4. In a saucepan beat egg yolks and sugar until creamy.
5. Add milk and cook over low heat until thickend, stirring constantly with a wooden spoon to avoid scorching.
6. Add vanilla and soaked gelatin. Stir until all the gelatin is completely dissolved. Do not boil.
7. Add tofu purée and mix thoroughly.
8. Place the saucepan into a large bowl filled with ice water that reaches half the height of the saucepan. Stir and cool until the egg-gelatin mixture begins to thicken. Do not let it become totally firm.
9. Meanwhile, whip heavy cream until stiff. Quickly fold into the thickened gelatin mixture. Mix until combined.
10. Rinse a 1½ qt. pudding mold with cold water and fill with the cream mixture to ¾ full. Keep the rest of the cream in the saucepan.
11. Dissolve instant coffee in 1 tablespoon of hot water. Add to the cream in the saucepan. Mix quickly and thoroughly.
12. Fill an icing bag with a 2-inch (5 cm) round nozzle with coffee cream. Insert the nozzle to the center of the vanilla cream and pipe slowly, until all the coffee cream is used. Vanilla cream will make its way automatically to the wall and coffee cream will stay in the center. Take out the nozzle gently to avoid the coffee cream coming out. Chill. Unmold dessert and serve.

# Steamed Chestnut Okara Pudding

Cold pudding with a hot chocolate sauce is a special fall treat.

## Ingredients:

10 oz. (300 g) chestnuts, peeled, cooked and drained
4 eggs
½ teaspoon salt
¼ cup (60 ml) chestnut syrup★
¼ cup (60 ml) salad oil
½ teaspoon vanilla extract
2 teaspoons baking powder
1½ cups (200 g) okara

## Method:

1. Dice ⅓ of the chestnuts and set aside. Purée the rest of the chestnuts in a blender.
2. Add eggs, salt, syrup, oil, vanilla and blend until smooth. Set aside.
3. Mix okara with baking powder in a bowl.
4. Add chestnut mixture and mix well. Stir in diced chestnuts.
5. Grease a quart mold or 8 muffin cups and fill to ¾ of the height with the okara-chestnut mixture.
6. Steam at high temperature about 45 minutes or until it feels elastic when lightly touched in center.
7. Unmold. Serve hot or cold with hot chocolate sauce.

★ Bring 1 cup (240 ml) water and ½ cup (120 g) sugar to a boil. Add peeled chestnuts and cook until soft. Cool in the syrup.

# Peach Pie

Try using other canned fruits, such as apples or pears, to create creamy fruit pies that will delight your family or guests.

**Ingredients:**
1 prepared pie shell (page 116)
2 eggs
1½ cups (300 g) mashed tofu
3 oz. (90 g) cream cheese
¾ cup (150 g) sugar
2 teaspoons cornstarch
¼ teaspoon salt
½ teaspoon cinnamon
1 tablespoon curaçao
8 canned peach halves, drained

**Method:**
1. Prebake pie shell at 350°F. (180°C.) for 45 minutes. Set aside.
2. Combine eggs, tofu, cream cheese, sugar, cornstarch, cinnamon, salt and curaçao in a blender until smooth.
3. Pour about 1 cup of the tofu filling into the pie shell. Distribute filling evenly over the bottom of the crust.
4. Arrange peach halves round sides up on top of the filling. Pour remaining filling around the peaches, leaving some of the surface of the peaches exposed.
5. Bake pie for about 50 minutes, or until a knife inserted in the pie comes out clean. Cool. Serve pie chilled for best flavor.

Makes one 9-inch (23 cm) pie.

# Tofu Fruit Shake

**Ingredients:**
½ cup (⅛ l) cold milk
⅓ cup (70 g) mashed tofu
¾ cup (150 g) chopped fruit (try banana, peaches, strawberries)
1 tablespoon sugar (or to taste)
⅛ teaspoon salt
A dash of vanilla
2–4 ice cubes

**Method:**
1. Put all ingredients in a blender. Mix until smooth.
2. Pour into a tall glass and enjoy!

Makes 1 large serving.

# Tofu Carrot Pie

Use commercially frozen pie shells or try the pie crust recipe on page 114.

**Ingredients:**
1 pie shell (9 inches, 23 cm)
Filling:
   2 cups (400 g) sliced cooked carrots, drained
   1 cup (180 g) packed brown sugar
   1 egg
   1½ cups (300 g) mashed tofu
   1 tablespoon cornstarch
   1 teaspoon freshly grated orange peel
   ¼ teaspoon nutmeg
   ½ teaspoon cinnamon
   ½ teaspoon ginger
   ½ teaspoon salt
   1 tablespoon curaçao (or 1 teaspoon vanilla extract)

**Method:**
1. Preheat oven to 350°F. (180°C.). Meanwhile, mix filling ingredients in a blender until smooth. Set aside.
2. Prebake pie shell 5 minutes, remove from oven to cool.
3. Pour tofu filling into pie shell.
4. Bake about 45 minutes or until knife inserted in center comes out clean.
5. Chill pie for at least 4 hours or overnight. Decorate with small carrots and parsley sprigs.

# Okara Fruit Tart

**Ingredients:** for 8-inch (20 cm), flan
  dish
For crust:
    ¼ cup (50 g) sugar
    ½ cup (100 g) butter
    1 cup (150 g) all purpose flour, packed
For topping:
    1 cup canned or stewed fruits like
       apricots, prunes, apples, rhubarb, sour
       cherries, etc., drained (½ lb., 250 g)
    1 stick (125 g) unsalted butter
    ½ cup (90 g) sugar
    2 eggs
    1 cup okara, packed
    ½ teaspoon rum flavor
For the form:
    1 teaspoon butter or shortening
    1 tablespoon all purpose flour
For glaze: (optional)
    ½ cup melted apricot jam (¼ lb., 120 g)

**Method:**
1. With a pastry blender mix all ingredients for crust.
2. Grease the flan dish and dust with flour.
3. Press the dough over the bottom of the dish and bake in preheated oven at 375°F. (190°C.) for 15 minutes.
4. Take out of the oven and let cool for 5 minutes. Cover the crust with drained fruit. Set aside.
5. Cream butter and sugar together. Add eggs one by one and blend thoroughly.
6. Loosen the lumps of the okara with your fingers and add to the egg mixture.
7. Add rum extract. Blend well. Pour over the fruit.
8. Bake in preheated oven at 375°F. (190°C.) for 30 minutes or until a toothpick inserted in the center of the topping comes out clean.
9. Unmold. Melt ½ cup apricot jam with 2 tablespoons of water over very low heat and brush the surface of the tart with it.

# Apple Cake ★

A great cake for picnics or lunch boxes!

**Ingredients:**
2 cups (280 g) all purpose flour
1½ teaspoons baking soda
1 egg
½ cup (⅛ l) salad oil
1 cup (200 g) mashed tofu
1 cup (170 g) brown sugar
2 teaspoons cinnamon
½ teaspoon salt
1 teaspoon vanilla extract
1 cup (150 g) chopped apples
1 cup (130 g) chopped nuts

**Method:**
1. In a large bowl combine the flour and baking soda. Set aside.
2. Combine egg, oil, tofu, sugar, cinnamon, salt and vanilla until smooth.
3. Combine the tofu mixture into the flour mixture. Do not overmix! Batter will be slightly stiff and lumpy. Stir in chopped apples and nuts.
4. Place batter in a greased 9 × 13-inch (22.5 × 32.5 cm) cake pan. Bake at 350°F. (180°C.) for about 35 minutes or until a toothpick inserted in the center of the cake comes out clean.
5. Serve the cake with a sprinkling of powdered sugar.

# Refrigerator Cheesecake

Garnished with fresh fruit this cheesecake makes a luscious, light and refreshing dessert.

**Ingredients:**
2 tablespoons gelatin
6 tablespoons water
⅓ cup (70 g) sugar
1⅔ cups (350 g) tofu
1¼ cups (300 ml) yogurt
1 package cream cheese (3 oz., 90 g)
½ teaspoon salt
1 teaspoon vanilla extract
1 crumb crust pie shell (page 115)
Fruit for garnish

**Method:**
1. Put gelatin in a custard cup and add the water. Melt the gelatin in a microwave oven, or over low heat. Set aside.
2. Combine sugar, tofu, yogurt, cream cheese, salt and vanilla in a blender until smooth.
3. Add the melted gelatin and blend until smooth.
4. Pour mixture into the crumb crust shell. Chill at least 4 hours, or overnight.
5. Before serving, garnish with fresh fruit.

Makes one 9-inch (23 cm) cheesecake.

# Tofu Cream Pudding

## Ingredients:
⅔ cup (80 g) non-fat dry milk powder
1¼ cups (250 g) tofu
1 teaspoon vanilla extract
¼ cup (60 ml) water
½ teaspoon salt
2 tablespoons cornstarch
½ cup (80 g) sugar
1⅔ cups (400 ml) cold water

## Method:
1. Mix tofu, milk, vanilla, water and salt together in a blender until smooth. Set aside.
2. In a saucepan, mix cornstarch and sugar. Add water and cook until clear and thick.
3. Add the tofu mixture to the cooked cornstarch and blend.

6 servings.

Keep leftovers covered in the refrigerator for up to 3 days.

# Frosty Peach Dessert

## Ingredients:
1 egg yolk
6 tablespoons sugar
3 tablespoons salad oil
¼ cup (50 g) butter or margarine
1 teaspoon vanilla extract
⅛ teaspoon salt
1½ cups (375 g) canned peaches, drained
1½ cups (300 g) mashed tofu

## Method:
1. Mix egg yolk, sugar, oil, butter, vanilla, salt and ½ cup of the drained peaches together in a blender until smooth. Pour into a storage container or metal bowl.
2. Stir in remaining peaches. Freeze until mushy (about 4 hours). If a softer frozen dessert is desired, let the mixture stand at room temperature for about 15 minutes before scooping into serving dishes.

Makes 6 servings.

# Chocolate Frozen Dessert

## Ingredients:
1½ cups (300 g) tofu
3 tablespoons salad oil
¼ cup (30 g) cocoa
½ cup (90 g) brown sugar
¼ cup (50 g) butter or margarine
⅛ teaspoon salt
1 teaspoon vanilla extract

## Method:
1. Mix all ingredients together in a blender until smooth.
2. Spoon tofu mixture into a storage container or metal bowl. Cover and freeze until mushy (about 4 hours).

Makes 6 servings.

## Note:
This dessert can be kept frozen about 1 month. If you desire a soft frozen treat, let mixture stand at room temperature for about ½ hour before serving.

# Strawberry Frozen Dessert

## Ingredients:
1 lb. (450 g) tofu
½ cup (90 g) sugar
3 tablespoons butter or margarine
¾ cup (250 g) strawberry jam
¼ cup (60 ml) salad oil
⅛ teaspoon salt
1 teaspoon vanilla extract

**Method:**

1. Mix all ingredients together in a blender until smooth.
2. Spoon tofu mixture into a storage container or metal bowl. Cover and freeze until mushy (about 4 hours).

Serves 8.

# Flaming Crêpes

**Ingredients:**

Batter for crêpe:
- 1 egg
- 1 cup (225 g) tofu
- ¼ cup + 1 tablespoon (75 ml) milk
- 1 tablespoon salad oil
- 1 tablespoon sugar
- ½ teaspoon vanilla extract
- ½ teaspoon baking powder
- ¼ teaspoon salt
- ⅔ cup (100 g) all purpose flour

Magic Sauce:
- ½ cup (100 g) butter
- ¼ cup (50 g) natural sugar
- 2 teaspoons grated orange rind
- ½ cup (120 ml) orange juice
- 1 teaspoon lemon juice
- ¼ cup (60 ml) orange-flavored liqueur
- 2 tablespoons brandy

**Method:**

1. Combine all ingredients for batter in a blender and blend until smooth. Let rest in refrigerator for 1 hour. Then follow the instructions for crepe making on page 112.
2. Sauce: Cream butter and sugar together until smooth. Add orange rind, orange juice and lemon juice.
3. Heat this mixture in a frypan or chafing dish. Dip the tofu crêpes into the sauce mixture and fold them into quarters. Push them to the edges of the pan.
4. Heat liqueur and brandy in a small pan, pour the warmed liqueur over the crêpes in the sauce and ignite

## Soft Spice Cookies

Omit the dried fruit and pipe dough through a pastry tube to form exquisite cookies for any holiday.

**Ingredients:**
1 egg
1 cup (200 g) mashed tofu
¾ cup (150 g) brown sugar
½ cup (⅛ l) salad oil
1 teaspoon ginger
1 teaspoon cinnamon
1 teaspoon vanilla extract
½ teaspoon nutmeg
½ teaspoon salt
1¾ cups (250 g) all purpose flour
½ teaspoon baking soda
1 cup (150 g) chopped dried fruit (raisins, prunes, apples, etc.)
1 cup (120 g) whole nuts (almonds, walnuts, cashews, etc.)

**Method:**
1. Mix first 9 ingredients together in a blender until smooth. Set aside.
2. Sift together flour and baking soda in a large bowl. Add tofu mixture. Dough will be sticky.
3. Stir in fruit.
4. Drop dough by teaspoonfuls on a greased baking sheet. Press a nut onto each cookie.
5. Bake at 350°F. (180°C.) for about 10 minutes or until cookies are brown around the edges. Cool cookies on a cooling rack.

Makes 2 to 3 dozens.

## Holiday Fruitcake

Much lower in calories, but just as delicious as the traditional Christmas cake.

**Ingredients:**
2 cups (280 g) all purpose flour
1½ teaspoons baking soda
1 egg
½ cup (⅛ l) salad oil

1 cup (200 g) mashed tofu
1 cup (180 g) brown sugar
2 teaspoons cinnamon
½ teaspoon salt
1 teaspoon brandy or vanilla extract
1 cup (160 g) preserved fruit, or fruitcake
   mix
1 cup (130 g) chopped nuts
½ cup (170 g) apricot jam for glaze
   (optional)

**Method:**
1. In a large bowl, combine flour and
   baking soda. Set aside.
2. Combine egg, oil, tofu, sugar, cinnamon,
   salt and brandy together in a blender until
   smooth.
3. Mix tofu and flour mixtures together until combined. Add fruit and nuts.
4. Place dough in a greased 1 quart ring
   mold or tube pan, or in muffin cups.
5. Bake at 350°F. (180°C.) for about 35 minutes (20 minutes for the muffin size
   fruitcakes) or until a toothpick inserted
   in center of cake comes out clean. Cool.
6. Wrap well, and store in refrigerator. Before serving melt the jam with a little water in a small saucepan and brush on cake
   surface.

Makes one large fruitcake.

# Sweet Potato Pie

Garnish pie with dallops of Tofu Whip
(page 117).

**Ingredients:**
1 prepared pie shell (page 114)
2 cups (400 g) cooked sweet potatoes,
   mashed
1 lb. (450 g) tofu
1 cup (240 ml) fresh orange juice
½ cup (126 g) butter or margarine
¾ cup (150 g) brown sugar
2 eggs
1 strip orange peel (½ × 1 inch,
   1.3 × 2.5 cm)
½ teaspoon salt
¼ teaspoon nutmeg

1 tablespoon cornstarch
1 teaspoon vanilla

**Method:**
1. Prebake pie shell 5 minutes at 350°F.
   (180°C.). Set aside.
2. Combine potatoes, tofu, juice, butter,
   sugar, eggs, orange peel, salt, nutmeg,
   cornstarch and vanilla in a blender until
   smooth.
3. Pour tofu mixture into pie shell and bake
   for about 35–40 minutes, or until a knife
   inserted in the center of pie comes out
   clean. Chill thoroughly before serving.

Makes one 9-inch (23 cm) pie.

# Okara Bonbons

Dip bonbons in melted chocolate for an
elegant candy.

**Ingredients:**
½ cup (125 g) peanut butter
⅓ cup (70 g) packed okara★
3 tablespoons honey
¼ cup (35 g) skim milk powder
(1 tablespoon cocoa, coconut, chopped nuts,
   or wheat germ for rolling.)

**Method:**
1. Mix peanut butter, okara, honey, and
   skim milk powder together until smooth.
   Dough should be stiff enough to roll into
   balls. If too sticky, add more skim milk
   powder.
2. Divide dough into halves. Blend cocoa
   into one half.
3. Break off pieces of dough of each flavor.
   Roll each piece into a 1-inch (3 cm) diameter ball. Or make bonbons of each
   flavor, or half and half.
4. Roll bonbons in cocoa, wheat germ,
   coconut, or chopped nuts.

Makes 25 candies.

★ If uncooked okara is used, heat it for
   about 15 minutes, stirring constantly with
   a wooden spatula. Do not let it burn. Let
   cool before use.

# Easy-to-Do Tofu Cheese Cake

Very easy and inexpensive but absolutely delicious. Bake just the filling in a buttered and sugared form, and you will have an exciting soufflé.

**Ingredients:** for 10-inch (24 cm) spring form
Crust:
    ½ cup (100 g) sugar
    ½ + ⅓ cup (200 g) butter
    2 cups (300 g) all purpose flour
Filling:
    1½ cups (300 g) tofu, lightly pressed
    1 can (397 g) sweetened condensed milk
    4 egg yolks
    2 tablespoons cornstarch
    ¼ teaspoon lemon extract
    Juice of 2 lemons
    4 egg whites

**Method:**
1. Preheat oven to 375°F. (190°C.).
2. Grease the bottom of a springform pan and dust with flour.
3. Blend crust ingredients thoroughly with a pastry blender or with fingers. Spread the dough over the bottom of the pan and press lightly with your palm.
4. Mix in a blender the first 6 ingredients for filling until very smooth. Set aside.
5. Beat egg whites until stiff. Pour tofu mixture over egg white and mix gently with a rubber spatula.
6. Pour filling onto the crust. Bake on the lowest oven rack for about 60–70 minutes. Let cool in the pan.

Serves 12–16.

# Coconut Tofu Dessert   ★

Serve this dessert with chilled brown sugar syrup.

**Ingredients:**
1¼ cups (300 g) tofu, drained
2 cups (½ l) milk
2½ cups (200 g) coconut flakes
½ cup (90 g) sugar
4 tablespoons (36 g) powdered gelatin, soaked in ¼ cup (120 ml) water
½ teaspoon vanilla extract

**Method:**
1. In a saucepan bring milk to a boil. Remove from heat.
2. Add coconut and let stand for 10 minutes. Press through a strainer into another saucepan. Discard the coconut.
3. Add sugar and soaked gelatin to the coconut milk and heat just till sugar and gelatin are dissolved. Do not boil.
4. Purée tofu in a blender and pour into the gelatin mixture. Add vanilla and mix thoroughly.
5. Rinse pudding mold about 5 × 4 × 3 inches (12 × 10 × 7 cm) with cold water. Fill with the tofu gelatin mixture. Chill.
6. Serve with cold brown sugar syrup.

Serves 4–5.

**Brown Sugar Syrup:**
1 cup (170 g) coarse brown sugar
1 cup (200 g) sugar
1 cup (¼ l) water
1 egg white

**Method:**
1. In a saucepan mix brown sugar, ½ cup (⅛ l) water and egg white with your fingers.
2. Add rest of the water and bring to a boil. Immediately reduce heat to low and cook slowly until the egg white foam becomes transparent. Strain through a cloth and chill. This syrup keeps in a airtight jar in refrigerator up to a month.

# Okara Carrot Cake

Very healthy, yet rich in taste.

**Ingredients:**
6 egg yolks
1 cup (170 g) brown sugar
½ cup (90 g) sugar
½ cup (70 g) flour
A pinch of cinnamon
A pinch of cloves
A pinch of salt
1 teaspoon baking powder
2 tablespoons kirschwasser
    or rum
3 medium-sized carrots (10 oz., 300 g),
    finely grated
2½ cups (240 g) packed okara★
6 egg whites

**Method:**
1. Preheat oven to 375°F. (190°C.). Beat egg yolks and brown sugar together until creamy. Set aside.
2. Sift together flour, spices, salt and baking powder.
3. Add dry ingredients to the egg yolk mixture. Mix thoroughly.
4. Crumble okara with your fingers until it is free of lumps. (★If okara is too wet, stir-fry it in a clean, ungreased frypan, until it is not damp anymore. Cool before using.)
5. Blend in kirschwasser. Add carrots and okara to the egg yolk mixture and mix well.
6. Beat egg whites with remaining sugar until stiff.
7. Fold in ¼ of the egg white into the okara mixture. Fold in the remaining egg white.
8. Grease and flour only the bottom of a springform. Fill with the batter, smooth the surface with a spatula and bake for about 40 minutes or until a toothpick inserted in center of the cake comes out clean.
9. Cool completely on a cake rack. Frost with melted chocolate and let harden.

# Okara Cake with Lemon Icing

Surprisingly light and refreshing.

**Ingredients:**
6 egg yolks
½ cup (90 g) brown sugar
½ cup (80 g) sugar
½ teaspoon vanilla extract
2 cups (240 g) okara★
½ cup (70 g) all purpose flour
1 teaspoon baking powder
Juice of ½ lemon
6 egg whites
For the icing:
    1 cup (130 g) powdered sugar
    2 tablespoons lemon juice

**Method:**
1. Grease the bottom of a springform 10-inch (26 cm) pan and dust lightly with flour.
2. Beat egg yolks and ½ cup brown sugar until creamy.
3. Add vanilla and lemon juice. Blend until smooth.
4. Sift flour and baking powder into the egg yolk mixture. Mix thoroughly.
5. Loosen the lumps of the okara with your fingers and add to the egg yolk mixture.
6. Beat egg whites with the remaining sugar until very stiff.
7. Fold in ¼ of the egg white to the egg yolk-okara mixture. Gently add the rest of the egg white to the okara mixture.
8. Fill the form with the batter and smooth the surface with a spatula. Bake in a preheated oven for 45 minutes.
9. Mix powdered sugar and lemon juice until blended. Spread the icing over the top surface of the cake.

★ If okara is very wet, beat another small egg and add to the dough before folding in egg white.

# Whole Wheat Cheese Rolls

**Ingredients:**
1 lb. (450 g) tofu
½ cup (120 g) butter or margarine
¼ cup (25 g) grated Parmesan cheese
1 teaspoon salt
2 cups (240 g) whole wheat flour
2 teaspoons baking powder
1 teaspoon oregano (optional)
¼ cup (25 g) grated Parmesan cheese for
  rolling dough

**Method:**
1. In a blender, combine tofu, butter, ¼ cup Parmesan cheese and salt until smooth. Set aside.
2. In a large bowl, mix whole wheat flour, baking powder and oregano. Add the tofu mixture. Dough will be soft and somewhat sticky. Divide dough into halves.
3. Sprinkle a sheet of wax paper with 2 tablespoons Parmesan cheese. Place ½ of the dough onto the wax paper. Sprinkle top of the dough with a little flour to keep dough from sticking to your hands. Flatten the dough to about ½ inch (12 mm) thick, and shape into a circle.
4. Cut the dough circle into 8 triangles and roll (wide end to tip). Curve into a crescent shape. Repeat with other half of dough.
5. Place rolls onto greased baking sheet and bake for about 20 minutes at 375°F. (190°C.) or until light brown and rolls are no longer gummy inside.

Makes 16 rolls.

# Chinnamon Buns

So easy even children can make them!

**Ingredients:**
1 lb. (450 g) tofu
¾ cup (150 g) butter or margarine
1 teaspoon salt
2 cups (300 g) all purpose flour
2 teaspoons baking powder
⅓ cup (70 g) brown sugar
1 teaspoon cinnamon
½ cup (60 g) chopped nuts
2 tablespoons butter or margarine

**Method:**
1. Mix tofu, 3/4 cup butter and salt together in a blender until smooth. Set aside.
2. In a bowl combine flour and baking powder. Add tofu mixture. Stir until blended. Dough will be soft and somewhat sticky. Set aside.
3. Combine brown sugar, cinnamon and nuts. Set aside.
4. On a floured surface, roll out tofu dough to form a rectangle about 3/4 inch (2 cm) thick.
5. Spread 2 tablespoons butter on the surface of the dough, sprinkle with the cinnamon-sugar mixture.
6. Roll up the rectangle (long side to long side) and cut into slices about 1 inch (2.5 cm) thick. Place the buns, cut side down, on a greased baking sheet so sides of buns barely touch.
7. Bake at 350°F. (180°C.) for about 30 minutes or until rolls are light brown and no longer doughy.
8. Serve buns hot or reheat before serving.

Makes 6 large or 12 small buns.

# Okara Banana Bread

This recipe also makes great muffins! Pour batter into muffin cups and bake about 20 minutes. Makes 12 muffins.

**Ingredients:**
½ cup (90 g) brown sugar
½ cup (125 ml) salad oil
¼ cup (65 ml) orange juice
3 small bananas
½ teaspoon salt
1 teaspoon vanilla extract
1 egg
½ cup (70 g) packed okara
1 teaspoon baking powder
½ teaspoon baking soda
1¾ cups (210 g) whole wheat pastry flour
    (or all purpose flour)
1 cup (140 g) chopped nuts
1 teaspoon grated orange rind

**Method:**
1. Mix first 7 ingredients in a blender until smooth. Pour into a large bowl.
2. Add remaining ingredients, stirring, only until combined. Batter will be thick and lumpy.
3. Pour batter into greased loaf pan and bake at 325°F. (160°C.) for about 45 minutes or until toothpick inserted comes out clean. Cool bread in the pan for 30 minutes, then remove from pan.

Makes one 3½ × 7½-inch (9 × 19 cm) loaf.

# Okara Blueberry Muffins

Okara gives a nutty taste to the muffins.

**Ingredients:**
1 egg
¼ cup (60 g) sugar
½ teaspoon salt
1 cup (¼ l) milk
¼ cup (60 ml) salad oil
½ teaspoon vanilla extract
⅔ cup (100 g) flour
1 tablespoon baking powder
½ cup (120 g) cornmeal
1 cup (140 g) okara
1⅔ cups (240 g) blueberries

**Method:**
1. Grease 12 muffin cups.
2. Sift flour and baking powder together.
3. Combine okara and cornmeal, until all the lumps have disappeared. Add to the flour.
4. Blend first 6 ingredients in a bowl. Add to the flour mixture. Mix just until combined.
5. Fold in blueberries.
6. Fill the muffin cups ⅔ full.
7. Bake in preheated oven at 375°F. (190°C.) for 30 minutes or until a toothpick inserted in the center comes out clean and the muffins are light brown. Serve hot with butter.

**Variations:**
Instead of blueberries use chunks of other acid fruits like tart apples, apricots, pitted sour cherries, plums, etc. or ⅔ cup finely cut nuts or dried fruits.

---

**How to dry okara
(for Thin Okara Cookies):**
Put 1 cup of okara into a large, clean frypan or wok. Heat slowly, stirring constantly with a wooden spoon or chopsticks to avoid burning. According to initial moisture content of okara, it will take 20–30 minutes until become light and fluffy okara—not sticky. If a fine grain is desired, such as required in the recipe "Thin Okara Cookies" sift through a metal colander.

You can also dry okara in an oven. Sprinkle okara on a baking pan and place in a 212°F. (100°C.) oven. Bake until okara is dry and "fluffy" looking. Do not burn the okara! Store the cooled dry okara crumbs in airtight container. You can keep the crumbs at room temperature for about 3 weeks.

# Gingerbread Cookies

An easy to handle dough that kids of all ages will love to roll out or mold into favorite shapes.

**Ingredients:**
1½ cups (250 g) brown sugar
1 cup (200 g) mashed tofu
½ cup (⅛ l) salad oil
½ cup (⅛ l) molasses
2 teaspoons ginger
2 teaspoons cinnamon
¼ teaspoon cloves
¼ teaspoon nutmeg
1 teaspoon salt
2 teaspoons baking soda
5½–6 cups (770–840 g) all purpose flour

**Method:**
1. Mix brown sugar, tofu, oil, molasses, spices, salt and baking soda together in a blender until smooth. Set aside.
2. In a large bowl, put flour.
3. Add tofu mixture to flour and mix until combined. Toward the end of mixing, dough becomes stiff, so you may want to use your hands.
4. Chill dough for 3 hours or overnight.
5. Place dough between 2 sheets of wax paper and roll out ⅛–¼ inch (3–8 mm) thick. Cut dough into desired shapes with a cookie cutter.
6. Bake at 350°F. (180°C.) on a greased cookie sheet for about 8 minutes, or until slightly brown around the edges, and cookies are no longer doughy.

Makes approximately 50–100 cookies depending on the size of the cookie cutter.

**Note:**
Cookies can also be molded into shapes free-hand style. Bake formed cookies as directed. These cookies keep for about a month in an airtight container.

# Chocolate Chip Cookies

Okara absorb humidity very fast. Keep the cookies that contain okara in an airtight container. If they have become soft, crisp them in a warm oven.

**Ingredients:**
⅔ cup (200 g) shortening or margarine
½ cup (90 g) sugar
1 egg
1 teaspoon vanilla extract
1 cup (140 g) flour
½ teaspoon baking soda
½ teaspoon salt (optional)
1½ cups (200 g) okara
1 cup (170 g) semi-sweet chocolate chips

**Method:**
1. Blend together shortening, sugar, egg, and vanilla.
2. Sift together flour, soda, and salt. Stir into the shortening mixture.
3. Stir in okara and blend until smooth. Add chocolate chips and mix again.
4. Drop by the teaspoonfuls 1 inch (3 cm) apart on ungreased baking sheet.
5. Bake at 400°F. (200°C.) about 10 minutes, or until lightly browned. Cookies should be soft.
6. Cool slightly before removing from baking sheet. Store in a tight lidded container.

Makes about 50 cookies.

# Thin Okara Cookies

These cookies tend to become soft. Keep them in a container with absorbent. When they are not crisp anymore bake them again for a short time.

**Ingredients:**
1 egg
¾ cup (150 g) butter
½ cup (90 g) sugar
1 teaspoon vanilla extract
1¼ cups (200 g) flour
2½ cups (100 g) dried okara★, sifted

**Method:**
1. Blend the first 4 ingredients.
2. Add flour and okara. Mix well.
3. Roll out to a very thin sheet (about ¹⁄₁₀ inch, 2.5 mm). Cut into squares (2 × 2 inches., 5 × 5 cm).
4. Bake on a well greased baking sheet at 375°F. (190°C.) about 10 minutes or until golden brown. Do not burn. Remove immediately from baking sheet and cool on cooling rack. Store in a tight covered container.

Makes about 60 cookies.

# Okara Honey Cookies

Bake only what will be eaten in a short time, for these cookies become soft very quickly.

**Ingredients:**
¼ cup (50 g) butter
¼ cup (50 g) sugar
2 tablespoons (25 g) honey
2 tablesppons heavy cream
Grated rind of ½ lemon
1½ cups (100 g) dried okara★

**Method:**
1. Blend first 5 ingredients.
2. Add okara and mix well until smooth.
3. Form a small ball about half the size of a golf ball. Press between your palms lightly to flatten it. Place the cookies about 2 inches (5 cm) apart on a greased baking sheet.

4. Bake at 350°F. (180°C.) about 20 minutes, until golden brown. Remove from baking sheet and cool on a cooling rack.

Makes about 20 cookies.

# Oatmeal Okara Cookies

These cookies freeze well after baking. Flatten cookies with a fancy glass bottom and they will be almost too pretty to eat!

**Ingredients:**
⅔ cup (165 ml) salad oil
1 egg
½ cup (110 g) brown sugar
½ cup (70 g) okara
½ teaspoon salt
½ teaspoon baking soda
1 teaspoon cinnamon
1 teaspoon vanilla extract
1 cup (140 g) all purpose flour
1½ cups (130 g) oatmeal
½ cup (70 g) chopped almonds

**Method:**
1. Thoroughly combine all ingredients.
2. Form dough into 1-inch (2.5 cm) balls and place on a greased cookie sheet allowing 1½ inches (3.5 cm) between balls. Flatten with bottom of greased and sugared glass.
3. Bake at 350°F. (180°C.) for about 10 minutes or until light brown. Cool cookies on a cooling rack.
4. Store cookies in an airtight container.

Makes about 30 cookies.

★ dried okara, see page 106.

# Okara Crêpes

Soyfood at its most romantic!

**Ingredients:**
Crêpes:
 2 eggs
 1⅓ cups (330 ml) milk
 ½ cup (70 g) okara,
 ⅔ cup (100 g) all purpose flour
 ½ teaspoon salt
 2 teaspoons sugar
 2 tablespoons salad oil

**Method:**
Crêpes:
1. Mix all crêpe ingredients together in a blender until smooth. Let batter rest 1 hour. If batter seems too thick add a little more milk by the tablespoonfuls.
2. Lightly oil a small frypan and heat until oil is hot. Pour a small amount of batter in the frypan and quickly rotate the pan until the batter covers the bottom of the pan.
3. Cook the crêpe until the bottom is light brown. Using a spatula loosen the edges of the crêpe and flip it over to brown the other side. Crêpe pan makes the work easier (see photo).
4. As the crêpes become done, stack them using a sheet of wax paper. Have crêpes covered to keep them from drying out.
5. Serve with favorite jam, honey, ice cream or follow the recipe for flaming on page 91.

Makes about 12 crêpes.

# Pancakes

Due to the difference in flours, you may have to adjust the amount of milk to make a pourable batter.

**Ingredients:**
1 egg
1 cup (200 g) mashed tofu
⅓ cup (80 ml) milk
1 tablespoon salad oil
1 tablespoon sugar
½ teaspoon vanilla extract
½ teaspoon baking powder
¼ teaspoon salt
⅔ cup (100 g) all purpose flour

**Method:**
1. Mix all ingredients together in a blender until smooth.
2. Pour about ¼ cup of pancake batter on a greased griddle or frypan and cook until done on both sides.
3. Serve hot with butter, syrup or fresh fruit.

Makes 6 pancakes.

# Easy Pie Crust

### Ingredients:
2 cups (280 g) all purpose flour
1¼ teaspoons salt
⅔ cup (160 ml) salad oil
3 tablespoons milk

### Method:
1. In a bowl combine flour and salt. Set aside.
2. Add milk to the oil directly in the measuring cup. Stir with a fork.
3. Slowly add the milk-oil mixture to the flour, stirring all the time with a fork. The pastry will be slightly crumbly, but should hold a shape when pressed with your fingers.
4. Press the pastry into a pie pan using fingers or roll pastry out between 2 pieces of wax paper, and transfer to pie pan.
5. Bake pie crust according to filling recipe.

Makes one 9-inch (23 cm) pie shell.

### Baker's Tip:
To keep a pie crust from becoming soggy, prebake the pie crust for 5 minutes at 350°F. (180°C.) before filling. Continue baking pie as recipe directs.

# Crumb Crust

**Ingredients:**
¼ cup (35 g) wheat germ
2 cups (100 g) dry bread crumbs
¼ cup (50 g) brown sugar
1 teaspoon cinnamon
2 tablespoons salad oil
3 tablespoons butter or margarine

**Method:**
1. Mix all ingredients together with your fingers until blended.
2. Press crumb mixture into pie plate. You may use all the crumbs for the shell, or make a thinner crust using only ¾ of the mixture reserving ¼ for a crumb topping for the pie.
3. Bake shell 5 minutes at 325°F. (160°C.). Cool crust before filling.

Makes one 9-inch (23 cm) pie crust.

**115**

# Short Crust

### Ingredients:
1⅔ cups (250 g) flour
½ cup (125 g) butter
1 egg
A pinch of salt
2 tablespoons cold water

### Method:
1. Sift flour in a bowl. Add butter, egg, salt and blend quickly with a pastry blender or with your fingers. Add water little by little. Form dough to a ball. Chill for 2 hours.
2. Press the dough against the bottom and wall of a pie pan using your fingers or roll out between 2 pieces of wax paper, and transfer to pie pan.
3. Cut off excess dough with a knife.
4. For a flat pastry crust place a round plate on the rolled dough and cut the dough off along the edge of the plate. Bake crust on a cookie sheet.

# Tofu Whip

Glorious on top of Tofu Carrot Pie!

**Ingredients:**
1½ cups (350 g) drained tofu
¼ teaspoon salt
3 tablespoons sugar
1 teaspoon vanilla extract
1 tablespoon salad oil

**Method:**
1. Mix all ingredients together in a blender until smooth.
2. Use as you would whipped cream.

Makes about 1½ cups topping.

**Note:**
Keep tofu whip covered in the refrigerator.

# Soy Whip

To make this whipped topping you can use your own homemade soymilk or purchased soymilk. Adjust the amount of oil to make the whip soft or firm.

**Ingredients:**
3 tablespoons rich soymilk (see page 122)
6 tablespoons salad oil
1 tablespoon sugar
A pinch of salt
½ teaspoon vanilla extract

**Method:**
1. Mix soymilk, 3 tablespoons of the oil, sugar, salt and vanilla together in a blender until smooth.
2. While blender is "on", slowly add the remaining oil in a thin stream until the whip has reached the consistency you desire. More oil will produce a thicker whip, less oil a more soft one.
3. Serve as you would regular whipped topping.

Makes about ½ cup.

# Home Style Tofu

Because fresh tofu tastes best, home made tofu is preferred by all tofu gourmets.

**Ingredients:**
1¾ cups (370 g) soybeans, washed
1½ to 1¾ teaspoons nigari★

**Method:**
1. Soak soybeans in 6 cups (1.5 l) water overnight. **(A)**
2. Next day, rinse the beans with fresh water, then drain.
3. In a large pot, bring 4 cups (1 l) of water to a boil. While water is coming to a boil, put 1 cup of the drained beans and 2 cups (½ l) of water in a blender and purée until smooth. **(B-D)**
4. Pour puréed beans into the boiling water in the pot. Turn off heat.
5. Continue puréeing the soybeans and add them to the contents in the pot.
6. After all the soybeans have been puréed, rinse the blender with 2 cups (½ l) of water and add it to the pot.
7. Boil the puréed soybeans (now called

"slurry") for 20 minutes. Stir from time to time to keep slurry from burning. If the liquid foams up, turn the heat down and stir with a wooden spoon to break up the foam. **(E)**
8. Wet a gauze cloth (or a clean tea towel) and place it in a colander placed over another large pot. This pot will collect the strained slurry.
9. Strain the cooked slurry through the gauze cloth by gathering up the corners of the cloth to form a bag. Using the bottom of a clean jar or wooden paddle, press as much soymilk as possible from the contents of the bag. **(F) (G)**
10. Rinse the first pot with 2 cups (½ l) water and add it to the bag's contents. Press again.
    **Note:** The bag holds soy pulp or "okara." Do not throw okara away. Cool it, then wrap and store it in the refrigerator or freezer. See index for recipes that use okara as an ingredient. **(H)**
11. Rinse the gauze cloth and set it aside for step 16.
12. Bring the soymilk to a boil, stirring constantly. Remove from heat. **(I)**
13. In a small bowl mix 1 cup (¼ l) water and 1½ teaspoons nigari. Using a back and forth motion, stir the soymilk with a wooden spoon. Add ⅓ of the nigari solution. Stir gently. Stand the wooden spoon in the center of the pot to stop the swirling motion of the soymilk. **(J)**
14. Sprinkle another ⅓ of the nigari solution over the top of the soymilk. Cover the pot and wait 3 minutes for curds to form.
15. After 3 minutes, stir milky portions in the pot and sprinkle the remaining nigari over

okara            soy milk      H

119

**I**

these areas. (If no milky portions remain go to step 16.) Cover the pot and wait another 3 minutes. **(K)**

16. Line the colander with the damp gauze cloth and rewet it. Place the colander in the sink for draining.

17. Gently stir the surface of the pot contents, then move the spoon under the top curds to free any of the uncurdled milk that may be below. At this point curds should be floating in a clear, yellow liquid (whey). If not, dissolve ¼ teaspoon nigari with 3 tablespoons water and sprinkle it over the uncurdled areas. Cover the pot and wait another 3 minutes. **(L)**

18. Gently ladle the curds into the lined colander on tofu box. **(M, M')**

19. Fold the gauze over the top of the curds. Place a salad plate on top of the curds, then press the top with a weight (canned goods work well). **(N, O, O')**

20. Drain for about 15 minutes, or longer for a more firm tofu. Remove the tofu filled colander from the sink.

21. Fill the sink with cool water. Remove the weight and invert the tofu on the plate, using the buoyancy of the water. Lift off the colander. Gently unwrap the tofu. Let the tofu cool in the water filled sink for about 10 minutes. Lift the tofu out of the water. Keep it in refrigerator in a colander with fresh water. **(P, Q, R)**

Enjoy your gourmet tofu fresh with shoyu (soy sauce), or use it in your favorite recipe.

★ Nigari: Available in most natural food shops.

**J**

**K**

**L**

M

O′

M′

P

N

Q

O

tofu R

# Kitchen Style Soymilk

To make soymilk you will need a large colander, a cloth for straining (any large loosely woven cloth will do), a blender, a clean jar and a large heavy bottomed pot.

**Ingredients:**
1 cup (210 g) soybeans

**Method:**
1. Wash soybeans and soak them overnight in about 1 and ½ cups (375 ml) water.
2. After soaking, rinse beans, drain well, and divide into two portions.
3. Wet the straining cloth and line the colander with it. Place the colander inside the pot. Set the pot in the kitchen sink.
4. Bring one large kettle of water to a boil. Keep it at a full rolling boil.
5. Using 3 cups (750 ml) of this boiling water, preheat the blender jar by pouring the water into the blender. (WARNING! If you have a plastic blender jar use only hot tap water.) Set this aside for a few minutes. Keep the remaining water at full boil.
6. Empty the blender jar and add one portion of the beans with 1 ¾ cups (430 ml) boiling water. Purée for 1 minute. Pour this hot purée into the lined colander. Continue with other half of the beans.
7. Grab corners of the straining cloth to form a bag, twist ends together. Using the bottom of the clean glass jar, press the soymilk from the okara.
8. Rinse the blender with ¾ cup (180 ml) boiling water and add this to the contents of the straining cloth. Press again.

okara

9. Cook the soymilk over low heat for 20 minutes. Stir often as soymilk has a tendency to burn.
10. Cool the milk quickly by placing the pot into cold water. Change the water frequently. Pour the cooled milk into clean jars or containers, cover and store in the refrigerator.

Makes about 1 quart.

**Note:**
This soymilk is like cream. Use it for making yuba (page 117), soy whip (page 118), in cooking, or dilute it with water 1 : 1.

# Kitchen Style Yuba

To make yuba you will need an oblong
enamel pan about 5 × 19 inches
(13 × 23 cm), or a heavy round frying pan.
This is used as a steaming container. To keep
the steaming container off the heat, you will
need a pan larger than your steaming container
so that you can make a double boiler-like
system. Fill the larger container with water,
place on the burner, and you are ready to go!

**Ingredients:**
Kitchen Style Soymilk (p.123)

**Method:**
1. Pour the soymilk into the steaming container to the depth of 1–2 inches (2.5–5
   cm). Heat the soymilk until it is steaming,
   but not boiling. Wait for a "skin" to form
   on the surface (about 7–10 minutes).
2. Using a knife, cut the "skin" loose from
   the edges of the pan, slip a premoistened
   chopstick under it and lift off the yuba.
   Drain the yuba for a few minutes. Place
   yuba on a plate if you are going to serve it
   immediately, or drape the sheet over a
   moistened bamboo basket to dry.

Makes about 15 sheets.

**Note:**
Leftover yuba can be wrapped loosely in
plastic wrap and stored in the refrigerator. It
can also be frozen or air dried until brittle,
then reconstituted at a later time.

Dried yuba

yuba

**How to reconstitute dried yuba:**
Moisten 2 dish cloths and wring out excess moisture. Spread one cloth on a table. Keep the other ready. Dip a sheet of yuba for a short time into cold water. Place it on the cloth. Proceed with other sheets. Cover all the yuba with the other cloth and let stand until yuba becomes pliable.

# How to Make Thick Agé at Home

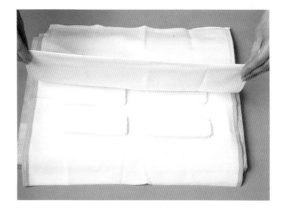

1. Cut tofu into ⅓-inch (8 mm) thick slices. Lay out on a dry cloth. Cover with another cloth and let stand for 20 minutes. Change the cloths and do the same over again until almost all the moisture is removed from the tofu.
2. Heat ample amount of vegetable oil (use partly sesame oil for a nut-like flavor) in a large pan to 356°F (180°C).
3. Let tofu slices slide into the oil 4 at a time and slowly deep-fry until golden. Be sure that the tofu is always covered with oil. Take them out and let oil drip.
4. Repeat the process till all the tofu slices are fried.
5. Heat oil to 446°F (230°C) and re-fry the tofu slices for a short time.

### Agé Pouches:

1. Pat with a rolling pin.
2. Cut agé in half crosswise. Insert your thumb into the opening and carefully pull apart the two layers. Douse with boiling water to remove excess oil.

# Agé Pouches

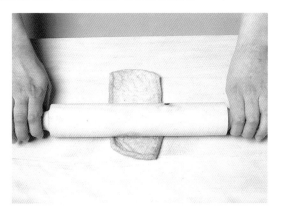

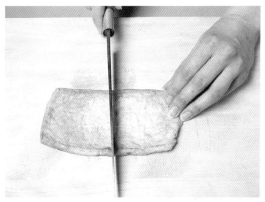

# Index of Recipes